THE AI SCRATCH CODE

▶ PLAYBOOK

A Beginner's Guide to Building Intelligent Systems

ROSEBROCK ADSON

The AI Scratch Code Playbook.

A Beginner's Guide to Building Intelligent Systems

ROSEBROCK ADSON.

Disclaimer:

Table of Contents

Introduction.

The world that we live in is being reshaped on a daily basis by artificial intelligence. The results of your search are powered by it; it removes spam from your inbox, it suggests what you should watch next, and it even analyzes data to save lives at times. However, here is the interesting part: artificial intelligence is not magic, nor is it something that is only available to highly skilled engineers who have advanced degrees. AI is constructed by employing straightforward ideas, unambiguous reasoning, and a series of procedures that are structured. In addition, the most exciting thing is that you can also learn how to make it.

Imagine for a moment that I informed you that you have the ability to comprehend, construct, and master the algorithms that are responsible for a virtual assistant, a self-driving car, or a predictive model. From this very moment on, you have the ability to transform yourself from a passive consumer of intelligent systems into a creator of those systems. All that is required of you is the appropriate direction and the bravery to get started.

The Promise and the Purpose.

Greetings, and thank you for visiting The AI Scratch Code Playbook: A Guide for Beginners to Constructing Intelligent Systems. This book is your path to creating and programming intelligent systems from the ground up. Whether you're brand new to coding or an ambitious coder trying to demystify AI, this tutorial will take you on a transforming trip.

You'll learn how AI works, not through abstract ideas, but with hands-on exercises and real-world situations. Step by step, we'll break down frightening topics into achievable tasks, leading you as you write your first lines of code and construct practical AI models. By the end, you'll not only comprehend AI—you'll be developing systems that can learn, adapt, and solve problems.

This isn't just a book; it's an opportunity to future-proof your talents in a world increasingly driven by AI. With every chapter, you'll gain practical tools, industry insights, and the confidence to create systems that go from basic functionality to cutting-edge innovation.

Connection.

Think about this: AI is transforming every industry it touches, from healthcare to entertainment, from education to business. It's not a trend—it's the future. But here's the secret: the most exciting element of this change isn't happening in research labs or corporate boardrooms. It's happening in the minds of curious individuals who dare to dig in, experiment, and create.

This book is for you—the thinker, the tinkerer, the dreamer who has wondered how AI works and how to be part of the tale. You don't need a plethora of experience to start, only a desire to learn. The trip may test you, but it will also thrill and empower you. By the end of this book, you won't just know AI—you'll own the capacity to develop it.

Getting prepared.

Are you ready to uncover your potential and take the first step toward creating intelligent systems? This is your time to remove barriers, turn curiosity into capability, and transform from a consumer of technology into its creator. Let's begin—what you build next could change the world.

A Vision for Your Future.

Picture this: you've created a program that can spot patterns in data, anticipate future trends, or even converse in natural language. The thing you once thought was impossible is now running on your computer, developed by your own hands. You've gone from being someone who only admired AI from afar to a confident creator capable of building solutions that make an effect.

The path ahead will teach you more than technical skills—it will educate you on how to think like a problem-solver, embrace creativity, and adapt to obstacles. The field of AI is not just about algorithms or code; it's about creativity, discovery, and bringing ideas to life. With this book as your guide, you'll have everything you need to start developing intelligent systems and writing your own chapter in the AI revolution.

Your Role in the AI Revolution.

It's no secret that artificial intelligence is altering sectors and opening new opportunities in technology, research, and business. But as powerful as AI is, its future hinges on one thing: individuals like you who are willing to learn, experiment, and push limits. The abilities you develop here won't just help you stay relevant—they'll position you to lead in a quickly evolving environment.

As you turn the pages of this book, you'll understand how AI works from the inside out. From core ideas like training algorithms and processing data to advanced techniques like building neural networks, this course will equip you with the tools to design your own intelligent systems. And because the information is designed step by step, you'll feel supported and empowered at every stage, no matter your starting point.

Why This Book?

What sets The AI Scratch Code Playbook distinct is its focus on accessibility and action. You won't be drowning in technical language or esoteric notions that seem out of reach. Instead, you'll get clear explanations, practical examples, and coding assignments that make complicated subjects simple and interesting. This isn't simply a manual—it's a playbook designed to inspire and challenge you while making AI approachable.

By the end of this book, you won't simply have learned about AI; you'll have constructed something tangible—an intelligent system that symbolizes your newfound talents and inventiveness. And more significantly, you'll have gained the confidence to continue researching, inventing, and experimenting in the exciting area of artificial intelligence.

The First Step.

Every journey starts with a single step, and this book is your first step into the AI frontier. It's normal to feel a combination of enthusiasm and uncertainty, especially if you're new to programming. But remember: every master was once a beginner. What is important is the willingness to start, learn, and keep going.

So as you go on this trip, ask yourself: What will you create? What problems will you solve? What ideas will you bring to life with AI? The possibilities are boundless, and they're waiting for someone like you to explore them.

Let's begin. The future of AI isn't simply something you'll read about—it's something you'll construct. And it all starts right here, with this book, and your curiosity to plunge in.

Chapter 1: Getting Started with AI Programming.

1.1 Understanding Artificial Intelligence Basics.

Artificial Intelligence, frequently termed AI, might sound sophisticated, but it's simply the ability of machines to accomplish activities that traditionally need human intelligence. These activities include things like recognizing voices, interpreting text, identifying photos, and making judgments based on data.

To understand AI better, it helps to split it down into smaller bits. At its heart, AI relies on computers and software to imitate some types of human reasoning. This can include thinking, problem-solving, and learning from experiences. For example, when you use a voice assistant like Siri or Alexa, it listens to your voice, processes the words you speak, and responds with helpful information or actions.

The Foundations of AI.

AI works because of three important components: data, algorithms, and computer power.

1. Data is the raw information that AI uses to learn and make judgments. For example, if an AI algorithm has to recognize cats in photos, it will need many pictures of cats to examine.

2. Algorithms are essentially step-by-step instructions that teach the computer what to do with the data. These instructions help the machine recognize patterns and solve issues.

3. Computing power refers to the speed and capability of the computer running the AI application. Modern AI requires fast processors to process vast volumes of data quickly.

These components work together to make machines "intelligent," allowing them to do specialized tasks effectively.

The Types of Artificial Intelligence.

There are different sorts of AI, but two key categories assist us in understanding how it works:

1. Narrow AI: This sort of AI is designed to accomplish one single task. It is the kind of AI we see most regularly nowadays. For example, a weather app that predicts the possibility of rain or an email filter that detects spam messages are both examples of limited AI. They are incredibly good at their tasks but cannot perform anything outside of their programming.

2. General AI: This type of AI would be able to execute any intellectual task that a person can do. It is an idea that scientists are still working toward, and it does not exist yet. The goal of general AI is to construct machines that can think, reason, and learn in a way that is similar to human intelligence.

Most of the AI applications we use today fall under the category of narrow AI.

Machine Learning and AI.

A key aspect of modern AI is something called machine learning (ML). Machine learning is how machines learn from data without being explicitly programmed. Instead of giving the computer explicit instructions for every possible case, machine learning allows the computer to figure things out on its own based on examples.

Here is an example: Imagine you want to teach a machine to recognize apples and oranges.

First, you would show the machine countless photographs of apples and categorize them as "apple."

Then, you would show photographs of oranges and identify them as "orange."

The system studies these examples and learns patterns, such as the form, color, and texture of apples and oranges.

When you show the computer a new picture, it can recognize whether it is an apple or an orange depending on what it learned.

This process of learning from examples is what makes machine learning so powerful.

Everyday Examples of AI.

Artificial intelligence is all around us, even if we don't always realize it. Some common instances include:

Search Engines: When you search for something online, AI helps locate the most relevant results for you.

Streaming Recommendations: Platforms like Netflix or Spotify propose movies, episodes, or music depending on your tastes, thanks to AI evaluating your activities.

Navigation Apps: Apps like Google Maps or Waze employ AI to provide instructions, recommend faster routes, and even alert you about traffic.

Online Shopping: When you shop online, AI helps recommend things you might enjoy, based on what you have looked for or purchased in the past.

These are just a few instances of how AI helps make routine jobs easier and more effective.

Why Learn AI Programming?

Learning AI programming is like opening the door to new possibilities. It allows you to design programs that can solve issues, automate processes, and even assist in improving lives. AI is employed in numerous industries, such as healthcare, finance, education, and entertainment. By grasping the principles of AI, you may start designing projects that are not only useful but also exciting.

This chapter will teach you the core principles you need to begin programming AI. From learning how computers interpret data to designing simple algorithms, you'll discover the key building blocks to start your AI adventure. Each part will focus on one step at a time, making the concepts easy to learn and apply.

This is your first step into the world of intelligent programming, where you'll learn how machines think and how to educate them to solve problems successfully. By understanding these basics, you'll be ready to take on more complex challenges in AI programming.

1.2 Setting Up Your Development Environment.

Before you start creating intelligent systems, it is vital to set up the tools you will require. These tools make it feasible to build, run, and test the code that powers artificial intelligence applications. Setting up your development environment might sound complicated, but with clear steps, it becomes straightforward and achievable.

What is a development environment?

A development environment is the place where you write and execute your code. Think of it as your digital workstation. It comprises software tools that let you design programs, check for faults, and run your AI models. A properly set-up environment guarantees your work is organized and efficient.

In AI programming, a good environment includes:

1. A programming language: This is the language you use to write instructions for the machine.

2. An editor or integrated development environment (IDE): This is the program where you write and test your code.

3. Libraries and frameworks: These are pre-written portions of code that facilitate AI programming.

4. A technique to handle dependencies: This guarantees all the tools and libraries you need operate together appropriately.

Now let's go through each of these components step by step.

Choosing a Programming Language.

The first thing you need is a programming language. Python is the most popular language for AI programming, and for excellent reasons:

It is beginner-friendly with simple and clear syntax.

It has a large range of libraries and frameworks built for AI.

It is utilized by experts; therefore, the skills you gain will be valuable in the real world.

If you don't already have Python installed on your computer, don't worry. It is free to download and install from its official website, python.org. Choose the latest stable version for your operating system (Windows, macOS, or Linux).

Installing an Editor or IDE.

Once you have a programming language, you need a place to write your code. This is where an editor or an Integrated Development Environment (IDE) comes in.

An editor is like a digital notebook for writing code, whereas an IDE offers extra tools to help you debug, test, and manage your code more efficiently. For novices, some popular options are:

1. VS Code (Visual Studio Code): A lightweight editor with important features like syntax highlighting, error detection, and extensions for Python.

2. PyCharm: A sophisticated IDE specifically developed for Python. It offers various tools to help you write, test, and debug AI programs.

3. Jupiter Notebook: A tool that enables you to create and run code in small portions, making it excellent for trying out ideas or learning step by step.

You can download these tools from their official websites. Most of them are free or have free versions.

Installing Python Libraries.

Python is powerful because of its libraries. A library is basically a toolkit filled with pre-written code that lets you do specific tasks. For AI development, some of the most important libraries include:

NumPy: Helps in handling numbers and performing calculations.

Pandas: Makes it easy to work with data in tables and spreadsheets.

Matplotlib and Seaborn: These are used for making graphs and displaying data.

Sickie-learn: Provides tools for machine learning tasks.

; PV: These are frameworks used for constructing and training neural networks.

To install these libraries, you will need a tool called pip. Pip is a package manager that comes with Python. You can use it to download and install libraries directly from the command line or terminal. For example, to install NumPy, you would type:

PIP INSTALL NUMPY.

You can install other libraries in the same way by substituting "numpy" with the name of the library you need.

Managing Dependencies.

When working on AI projects, you could employ many libraries and tools that depend on each other. Managing these dependencies is critical to avoid conflicts or problems.

One approach to solving this is by employing virtual environments. A virtual environment is like a separate workspace where you can install only the tools and libraries you need for a certain project. This keeps your projects grouped and assures that upgrades to one library won't break another project.

To construct a virtual environment, you can use Python's built-in utility called venv. Here are the steps:

1. Open your command line or terminal.

2. Navigate to the folder where you wish to construct your virtual environment.

3. Type the following command:

Python -m venv myenv.

Replace "myenv" with the name you wish for your virtual environment.

4. Activate the virtual environment:

On Windows:

myenv\Scripts\activate.

On macOS/Linux:

Source myenv/bin/activate.

When the virtual environment is running, you can install libraries without affecting the rest of your system.

Testing Your Environment.

Once everything is set up, it's a good idea to test your development environment to make sure everything is operating appropriately.

1. Open your editor or IDE.

2. Create a new Python file (for example, test.py).

3. Type the following code:

Import numpy as np.

print("Your environment is ready!")

4. Run the file. If the message "Your environment is ready!" appears, it means your setup is working.

Staying Organized.

As you start working on AI projects, keeping your files and tools organized will save you time and frustration.

Create a dedicated folder for each project.

Name your files and folders clearly so you can find them later.

Keep notes on which libraries and versions you used for each project.

This form of organizing helps make your work easier to handle, especially as your tasks grow more complex.

Moving Forward.

With your development environment set up, you are now ready to start programming. Each tool and library you've installed will play a crucial role as you write code and develop AI models. By following these steps, you have built a workspace where you may experiment, learn, and construct intelligent systems with confidence.

1.3 Key Tools and Languages for AI Projects.

Artificial intelligence is a fascinating field that relies on a combination of tools, languages, and frameworks. These elements simplify the process of designing intelligent systems and allow programmers to focus on addressing challenges. Understanding the most commonly used tools and languages can help you make educated selections as you start working on AI projects.

Programming Languages for AI.

Programming languages are at the heart of AI development. They allow you to write the instructions that a computer follows to perform tasks. While numerous languages can be used for AI, several are more typically used due to their features, community support, and availability of libraries.

"Python"

Python is the most common language for AI programming. It is commonly used because of its simple syntax, which makes it beginner-friendly. Python also includes a huge variety of tools and frameworks specifically intended for AI workloads.

Key benefits of Python include:

Readable and concise code, which is easy for beginners to understand.

A vast community of developers makes it easy to get help or resources.

Compatibility with major AI libraries like TensorFlow, PyTorch, and Scikit-learn.

R.

R is another language commonly used in AI, particularly for jobs involving statistics and data analysis. It is powerful for making visuals and processing massive datasets. While not as beginner-friendly as Python, R is highly useful for jobs that require complex statistical modeling.

"JavaScript"

JavaScript has gained prominence in AI development because it works seamlessly in web applications. With tools like TensorFlow.js, you can develop and run AI models directly in a web browser. This makes JavaScript a wonderful choice for applications that need to communicate with users online.

Other Languages.

Other languages, including Java, C++, and Julia, are also utilized in AI, depending on the project requirements.

Java is trustworthy for large-scale systems, especially in enterprise contexts.

C++ is utilized where performance is crucial, such as in game AI.

Julia is designed for numerical computing and is garnering attention for AI applications.

Libraries and Frameworks.

Libraries and frameworks are pre-written portions of code that facilitate AI development. They save you time and effort by providing tools for typical activities like data processing, training models, and developing neural networks.

"TensorFlow"

TensorFlow is a prominent open-source library established by Google. It is commonly used for machine learning and deep learning tasks. TensorFlow facilitates creating and training sophisticated neural networks, making it a favorite among researchers and developers.

"PyTorch"

PyTorch is another excellent library for AI, developed by Facebook. It is notable for its flexibility and ease of use, especially for deep learning. PyTorch is typically preferred by novices since it is more intuitive compared to TensorFlow.

"Scikit-learn"

Scikit-learn is a library that focuses on traditional machine learning algorithms, such as decision trees, support vector machines, and clustering approaches. It is simple to use and works well with other Python modules like NumPy and Pandas.

"Keras"

Keras is a high-level library that operates on top of TensorFlow. It provides a user-friendly interface for constructing and training deep learning models. Keras streamlines the process of developing neural networks, making it perfect for individuals new to AI programming.

"NumPy and Pandas"

NumPy and Pandas are key libraries for data manipulation and analysis.

NumPy helps with numerical computations, such as working with arrays and executing mathematical operations.

Pandas makes it easier to organize and analyze structured data, such as tables and spreadsheets.

"Matplotlib and Seaborn"

Matplotlib and Seaborn are libraries used for data visualization. They allow you to construct charts, graphs, and plots to better comprehend your data. These techniques are particularly useful when evaluating patterns or trends in datasets.

Tools for Managing Projects.

In addition to languages and libraries, certain technologies help manage AI projects more successfully.

Jupyter Notebook.

Jupyter Notebook is a commonly used application for developing and running Python programs. It allows you to separate your code into sections and run them one at a time. This is very beneficial when working on data analysis or testing AI models. Jupyter Notebook also supports putting notes and visualizations directly alongside your code.

Integrated Development Environments (IDEs).

IDEs provide an environment for authoring and testing code. Popular options for AI programming include:

PyCharm: A feature-rich IDE specifically built for Python development.

VS Code: A lightweight editor with additions for Python and AI libraries.

Version Control Systems.

Version control solutions allow you to track changes in your code and work with others. Git is the most prevalent technology for version control, and GitHub provides a platform for sharing and managing code repositories.

Cloud Platforms for AI.

Many AI projects demand huge quantities of processing power, especially when working with deep learning. Cloud platforms give the necessary resources without the need for pricey hardware.

Google Colab.

Google Colab is a free environment for running Python programs, notably AI experiments. It gives access to GPUs (Graphics Processing Units) and TPUs (Tensor Processing Units), which speed up the training of AI models.

Amazon Web Services (AWS).

AWS offers a number of tools and services for AI development. It is often used for deploying AI models in real-world applications.

Microsoft Azure.

Azure is another cloud platform that gives resources for AI programming. It supports machine learning, data analysis, and model deployment.

IBM Watson.

IBM Watson offers resources for constructing AI models, particularly for natural language processing and decision-making systems.

Data Sources and Tools.

AI initiatives generally rely on data to train models. Having access to high-quality data is vital for success.

Public Datasets.

Many organizations provide free datasets for AI development. These datasets span a wide range of topics, from photos and text to medical and financial data. Examples of popular public datasets include:

ImageNet: A big library of tagged photos for computer vision tasks.

Kaggle: A site that hosts datasets, tournaments, and learning materials for AI.

UCI Machine Learning Repository: A repository of datasets for machine learning research.

Data Cleaning Tools.

Data cleaning is the process of preparing raw data for usage in AI models. Tools like Python's Pandas module can help remove errors, fill in missing values, and organize data into a readable manner.

- **Hardware for AI.**

While most starting AI projects may be done on a regular PC, sophisticated ones like deep learning may require specialized gear.

GPUs.

Graphics Processing Units (GPUs) are faster than normal CPUs for AI workloads, especially when training huge models. Many cloud platforms provide access to GPUs, so you don't need to acquire one.

TPUs.

Tensor Processing Units (TPUs) are hardware accelerators designed exclusively for AI workloads. They are often employed in Google's cloud services.

Single-Board Computers.

Single-board computers like Raspberry Pi can run modest AI models and are excellent for applications requiring robotics or IoT (Internet of Things).

Understanding these tools and languages is the foundation for starting your AI programming adventure. With the necessary resources in place, you will have everything you need to create and test intelligent systems.

Chapter 2:

Foundations

of Intelligent

Systems.

2.1 Algorithms and Data Structures for AI.

When designing intelligent systems, knowing algorithms and data structures is vital. These are the essential building pieces that allow computers to solve problems efficiently. Whether you are working on a tiny project or a huge AI system, having a good grasp of how algorithms and data structures work can help you write better, faster, and more effective code.

What Are Algorithms?

An algorithm is a step-by-step technique for solving a problem or accomplishing a task. It is a series of instructions that tells the computer how to achieve a given goal. Algorithms are at the heart of most AI systems, as they specify how tasks such as learning, decision-making, and problem-solving are carried out.

For example, in a recommendation system (like the ones used by Netflix or Amazon), an algorithm gathers user preferences and then processes that information to suggest movies, shows, or purchases. The algorithm might look at patterns in past behavior, other similar users, or the ratings that a user has given to various goods.

Algorithms are often meant to be efficient and accurate. An efficient algorithm completes a task in the least amount of time and with the least number of computational resources. In AI, efficiency can dramatically affect the performance of a model or system, especially when dealing with huge datasets or complex calculations.

Key Types of Algorithms in AI.

There are various sorts of algorithms typically employed in AI programming. Some of the most important include:

Search Algorithms.

Search algorithms are used to identify specific information or solve problems by searching through a list of probable solutions. These algorithms are vital in AI applications like path finding in games or decision-making in automated systems.

For example, in a game like chess, a search algorithm might help software pick the best move by examining all possible movements and determining which one leads to the best conclusion. Some common search algorithms include:

Breadth-First Search (BFS): Explores all feasible solutions level by level.

Depth-First Search (DFS): Explores a path to its fullest before retracing and trying another path.

Sorting Algorithms.

Sorting is the process of putting data in a certain order, such as alphabetical or numerical order. Sorting is a key step in many AI systems, especially when working with huge datasets. Sorting helps to speed up searches, optimize decision-making, and arrange information efficiently.

Common sorting algorithms include:

Bubble Sort: Repeatedly compares neighboring elements and swaps them if they are in the wrong order.

Quick Sort: Divides the data into smaller sub-arrays and sorts them individually, leading to faster performance than other sorting algorithms.

Classification Algorithms.

Classification is a form of supervised learning technique that categorizes data into predetermined classes. In AI, classification algorithms are employed in tasks including picture recognition, sentiment analysis, and email filtering. For instance, a classification algorithm can be trained to discriminate between spam and non-spam emails by examining the content of the messages.

Some well-known classification algorithms include:

Decision Trees: These use a tree-like structure to model decisions and their possible consequences.

K-Nearest Neighbors (KNN): This algorithm allocates a data point to the class that is most prevalent among its neighbors.

Support Vector Machines (SVM): This algorithm finds the best boundary (hyperplane) that separates various classes.

Regression Algorithms.

Regression is another sort of supervised learning technique used to predict continuous values. For example, regression can be used to forecast the price of a house based on its size, location, and other parameters.

Some common regression algorithms are:

Linear Regression: Models the relationship between a dependent variable and one or more independent variables by fitting a straight line to the data.

Polynomial Regression: A more advanced version of regression that models the relationship using a polynomial equation.

Clustering Algorithms.

Clustering is a type of unsupervised learning algorithm used to group data into clusters or groups based on similarities. Unlike classification, clustering does not require labeled data. It is utilized for activities like consumer segmentation or anomaly detection.

Some common clustering algorithms include:

K-Means: Divides data into k clusters by minimizing the distance between the data points and the center of each cluster.

Hierarchical Clustering: Builds a tree-like structure of clusters, which can be useful for understanding relationships in the data.

Data Structures: The Foundation of Organizing Data.

In AI programming, data structures are used to store and arrange data in a way that makes it easy to access and alter. Choosing the correct data structure is critical for the performance and efficiency of your algorithm.

Data structures help to store and arrange data in ways that algorithms can use fast and readily. They can make it easier to conduct operations like searching for certain objects, sorting data, or adding and removing elements.

Here are some popular data structures used in AI programming:

Arrays and Lists.

Arrays and lists are the basic data structures used to hold a collection of elements. Both are linear structures that allow you to store elements in an ordered way. The key distinction is that arrays are fixed in size, while lists are dynamic, meaning they can expand or shrink as needed.

Arrays and lists are used to store data that needs to be processed sequentially, such as lists of numbers, text, or images. For example, in image processing, a picture might be represented as an array of pixel values.

Linked Lists.

A linked list is another sort of linear data structure, but it contains data elements in nodes, where each node points to the next one. Linked lists are excellent when you need to insert or remove items regularly, as they allow for rapid adjustments.

However, linked lists are less efficient than arrays when you need to access specific elements because you must traverse the list from the beginning.

Stacks and Queues.

Stacks and queues are forms of data structures that store data in certain orders.

Stack: Follows the Last In, First Out (LIFO) principle. The last element added is the first one to be withdrawn. Stacks are utilized in tasks like evaluating expressions or keeping track of recursive function calls.

Queue: Follows the First In, First Out (FIFO) concept. The first element introduced is the first one to be withdrawn. Queues are useful in circumstances where activities need to be processed in the order they come, such as in scheduling work for a computer's CPU.

Trees.

A tree is a hierarchical data structure that consists of nodes connected by edges. Each tree has a root node, and every other node is a child of another node. Trees are very effective for depicting hierarchical relationships, such as organizational hierarchies or family trees.

In AI, trees are widely employed in decision-making systems, where each node represents a decision, and the branches represent probable outcomes. A unique sort of tree, the binary tree, is often employed in search methods like binary search.

Hash Tables.

A hash table (or hash map) is a data structure that contains key-value pairs. Hash tables allow you to rapidly look up data based on a key, which makes them suitable for applications like searching for specific objects in vast databases. For example, you might use a hash table to store a user's information and get it by their unique user ID.

Hash tables are widely used in AI for activities that demand fast lookups, such as indexing databases or implementing algorithms that rely on speedy retrieval of data.

Graphs

Graphs are data structures used to depict relationships between items. A graph consists of nodes (sometimes called vertices) and edges that connect the nodes. Graphs are commonly used in AI to model networks, such as social networks, transportation systems, or the relationships between different things in a recommendation system.

Graphs can be used to solve problems like determining the shortest path between two points or discovering patterns in data. Algorithms like Dijkstra's algorithm or the A* algorithm are routinely employed to work with graphs.

The Role of Algorithms and Data Structures in AI.

Algorithms and data structures work hand in hand to handle and analyze data efficiently. For example, if you have a vast dataset and need to uncover certain patterns or predictions, you may use an algorithm like K-Nearest Neighbors (KNN) in combination with data structures like arrays or hash tables to make the process faster and more efficient.

By understanding how algorithms and data structures operate together, you may develop intelligent systems that handle problems in the most efficient way feasible. This combination of algorithms and data structures is what enables AI to make decisions, learn from data, and carry out tasks with extraordinary accuracy.

Having a strong foundation in algorithms and data structures will allow you to tackle increasingly complicated challenges and construct more advanced AI systems as you continue to study and grow in the field.

2.2 Introduction to Machine Learning Concepts.

Machine learning is a discipline of artificial intelligence that focuses on constructing algorithms capable of learning from data. Unlike traditional programming, where a programmer directly writes code to execute certain tasks, machine learning allows computers to learn from experience and improve their performance over time. This part will teach the core concepts of machine learning and help you understand how it fits into the world of intelligent systems.

What Is Machine Learning?

At its foundation, machine learning is about teaching computers to spot patterns and make judgments based on data. When a computer learns, it recognizes relationships and patterns within a set of input data and then uses that knowledge to make predictions or judgments without needing explicit programming.

Think of it as teaching a youngster how to distinguish animals. At first, the child might not know what an elephant or a dog looks like. However, by showing them several photographs of elephants and dogs, the toddler begins to notice patterns. After some time, the child can look at a fresh picture and accurately determine whether it's an elephant or a dog. In a similar way, machine learning algorithms evaluate data to detect patterns and then apply that knowledge to new scenarios.

Types of Machine Learning.

Machine learning is often classified into three primary categories: supervised learning, unsupervised learning, and reinforcement learning. Each category uses distinct techniques to learn and is suited to different types of challenges.

1. Supervised Learning.

Supervised learning is the most prevalent method of machine learning. In this strategy, the machine is presented with labeled data, which implies the correct responses are already known. The algorithm is then trained to recognize patterns in the data that correspond to the correct answers.

For example, if you were building a machine learning model to classify pictures of animals, you would provide the system with a dataset of images that are already labeled as "dog," "cat," or "elephant." The machine learns from these labeled examples and builds a model that can predict the label for new, unseen images.

Supervised learning is often used for tasks like:

Classification: Predicting categories or labels (e.g., recognizing spam emails or assessing if a customer is likely to buy a product).

Regression: Predicting continuous values (e.g., anticipating house prices based on factors like size and location).

2. Unsupervised Learning.

In unsupervised learning, the machine is fed data without any labeled replies. The goal is for the machine to detect patterns, groupings, or correlations within the data on its own.

One typical approach of unsupervised learning is clustering, where the system divides data into clusters of similar entities. For example, you could use clustering to categorize clients based on their shopping behavior. Even when the groups aren't named, the machine might nevertheless find natural groupings, such as clients who commonly buy the same types of things.

Another strategy in unsupervised learning is dimensionality reduction, where the machine minimizes the number of features in the data while maintaining the critical information. This is beneficial when dealing with large datasets that contain too many characteristics (variables), making it difficult to interpret or visualize the data.

Unsupervised learning is typically used for projects like:

Clustering: Grouping comparable items together (e.g., consumer segmentation).

Anomaly detection: Identifying odd patterns in the data (e.g., fraud detection).

Dimensionality reduction: Simplifying huge datasets while keeping significant aspects (e.g., displaying complex data).

3. Reinforcement Learning.

Reinforcement learning is a sort of machine learning where an agent learns to make decisions by interacting with an environment. The system receives input in the form of rewards or penalties based on its behaviors, and the goal is to maximize the total reward over time.

Imagine a robot traveling through a maze. Each time the robot takes a correct step towards the goal, it receives a tiny reward. If it makes an incorrect turn, it can earn a penalty. Over time, the robot learns which behaviors lead to the most rewards and becomes better at finding the quickest way to the goal.

Reinforcement learning is widely used for tasks like:

Game playing: Training AI to play games such as chess, Go, or video games.

Robotics: Teaching robots to accomplish tasks through trial and error.

Autonomous vehicles: Training self-driving automobiles to make decisions on the road.

Key Concepts in Machine Learning.

Now that we've looked at the many types of machine learning, it's crucial to grasp some of the key principles that drive machine learning algorithms. These concepts are fundamental to designing successful and efficient models.

1. Training and Testing.

In machine learning, the process of constructing a model typically involves two phases: training and testing.

Training: During the training phase, the machine learning model is fed data and learns from it. This data is used to alter the model's parameters so that it can make better predictions or judgments.

Testing: Once the model is trained, it is tested on new, unseen data to see how well it works. The testing phase helps to analyze whether the model is overfitting (learning the training data too well) or underfitting (failing to capture the patterns in the data).

Having separate training and testing data is critical because it ensures that the model doesn't only memorize the training data but can generalize its expertise to make correct predictions on new data.

2. Features and Labels.

In supervised learning, data is often represented as a set of features and labels.

Features: Features are the input variables or properties utilized to produce predictions. For example, in a property price prediction model, features can include the number of bedrooms, the size of the house, and the location.

Labels: Labels are the goal values that the model tries to forecast. In the housing pricing example, the label would be the actual price of the house.

In unsupervised learning, there are no labels, and the model tries to uncover patterns or groups within the characteristics.

3. Overfitting and Underfitting.

Overfitting and underfitting are common difficulties in machine learning that impair the model's performance.

Overfitting: Overfitting occurs when a model learns the training data too well, capturing not only the underlying patterns but also the noise and random fluctuations. This leads to poor performance on new, unknown data since the model has become overly specialized to the training data.

Underfitting: Underfitting happens when a model fails to learn the underlying patterns in the training data. This results in poor performance both on the training data and on new data.

The idea is to strike a balance between overfitting and underfitting. This can be performed by applying techniques like cross-validation, regularization, and altering the complexity of the model.

4. Model Evaluation.

Once a model has been trained and tested, it's crucial to evaluate its performance. This review helps to determine how well the model is doing and whether any adjustments are needed.

Several measures are routinely used to evaluate machine learning models:

Accuracy: The percentage of true predictions made by the model.

Precision: The fraction of optimistic predictions that are really correct.

Recall: The fraction of actual positive cases that the model properly recognizes.

F1 Score: The balance between precision and recall, especially when dealing with imbalanced datasets.

These metrics are used to measure how effectively the model is functioning and whether it is ready to be deployed in real-world applications.

Why Is Machine Learning Important?

Machine learning has become a vital tool for solving difficult problems across many areas, including healthcare, finance, marketing, transportation, and entertainment. By enabling computers to learn from data, machine learning allows us to design intelligent programs that can adapt to new conditions, improve over time, and make judgments based on large volumes of information.

From self-driving cars that learn to negotiate difficult traffic scenarios to personalized recommendation systems that forecast what movies you would like, machine learning is already revolutionizing industries and our daily lives. As the field continues to evolve, the potential applications for machine learning are practically infinite.

Machine learning also plays a vital part in the creation of intelligent systems. By leveraging data to drive decision-making and boost performance, machine learning provides the backbone for designing systems that can learn, adapt, and do activities that were long thought to be exclusive to people.

2.3 Discovering Neural Networks and Deep Learning.

Neural networks and deep learning are fundamental to the creation of intelligent systems. These techniques are inspired by the way the human brain analyzes information, and they have transformed the field of machine learning. In this chapter, we will introduce the basic ideas of neural networks and deep learning and explain how they lead to the formation of intelligent systems capable of learning, reasoning, and decision-making.

What Is a Neural Network?

A neural network is a model developed to imitate the way the human brain operates. It is made up of layers of interconnected nodes, which are referred to as "neurons." These neurons work together to analyze information and make decisions based on the input they receive. In a way, a neural network is a reduced, mathematical counterpart of a biological brain.

Each neuron in a neural network performs a fundamental task: it accepts input, processes that information using weights and biases, and provides an output. The output is subsequently passed on to the next layer of neurons. This process is continued over numerous levels until a final result is created.

Think of a neural network like a relay race. Each runner (neuron) in the race gets the baton (data) from the previous runner and passes it on to the next. The baton gets passed through multiple runners until reaching the finish line, when the result (output) is determined. The better each runner (neuron) performs, the faster and more accurately the race (or process) is completed.

The Structure of a Neural Network.

A neural network consists of three basic types of layers: the input layer, the hidden layers, and the output layer.

Input Layer: This is where the data enters the neural network. Each neuron in the input layer represents an aspect of the data. For example, if the network is processing photos, each neuron might represent a pixel of the image.

Hidden Layers: These are the layers between the input and output layers. They execute most of the work and are responsible for learning patterns in the data. A neural network can have one or more hidden layers, and the more layers there are, the more sophisticated the model gets.

Output Layer: This is where the ultimate forecast or judgment is made. In a classification challenge, the output layer could comprise neurons that represent distinct classes. In a regression issue, it might comprise a single neuron representing a continuous value.

Each link between neurons has a weight, which regulates the strength of the signal between two neurons. The model learns to change these weights during the training process to make more accurate predictions.

How Do Neural Networks Learn?

The process of training a neural network involves altering the weights and biases to increase the accuracy of the network's predictions. This is often done using a technique called backpropagation, paired with an optimization method like gradient descent.

Backpropagation.

Backpropagation is a method used to determine the error in the network's output and propagate that error back through the network to change the weights and biases. When a neural network makes a prediction, it compares the prediction to the actual result. The difference between these values is known as the "error." The goal is to minimize this error so that the network can make better predictions in the future.

Backpropagation works by sending the mistake backward through the network, from the output layer to the input layer, and modifying the weights at each neuron along the way. By doing this, the network learns from its mistakes and gradually improves its performance.

Gradient Descent.

Gradient descent is an optimization technique used to discover the values of the weights and biases that minimize the error. It operates by modifying the weights in small stages, based on the gradient of the mistake with regard to the weights. The gradient is essentially the slope of the error function, and it tells the algorithm which direction to move in to lower the error.

The gradient descent process starts with random initial values for the weights and iteratively adjusts them to minimize the error. Over time, the network "learns" from the data and becomes better at making predictions.

What Is Deep Learning?

Deep learning is a branch of machine learning that focuses on neural networks with several layers. These deep neural networks, often referred to as deep neural networks (DNNs), are capable of learning from large amounts of data and making complex decisions. Deep learning models are especially useful when the data is unstructured, such as images, audio, or text.

While traditional machine learning models might only have a few layers, deep learning models can have dozens or even hundreds of layers. This allows deep learning models to capture complex relationships in the data and make highly accurate predictions.

Why "Deep"?

The term "deep" refers to the number of layers in the neural network. The more layers a network has, the deeper it is. These layers allow the network to learn increasingly complex representations of the data.

For example, in an image recognition task, the first few layers of the network might learn to detect simple features like edges and colors. As the data moves through deeper layers, the network might learn to recognize more complex features like shapes, objects, and scenes. By the time the data reaches the output layer, the network is capable of making a sophisticated prediction, such as identifying the object in the image.

Applications of Neural Networks and Deep Learning.

Neural networks and deep learning have become essential tools in many areas of artificial intelligence. Their ability to learn from large amounts of unstructured data makes them particularly useful for complex tasks that are difficult for traditional machine learning models to handle. Some of the most common applications include:

1. Image Recognition.

Deep learning models are widely used in image recognition tasks, where the goal is to identify objects, people, or scenes in images. For example, a neural network might be used to detect faces in photos or to identify objects in autonomous vehicles' surroundings. Deep learning has also enabled the development of tools like facial recognition systems and automatic image tagging.

2. Natural Language Processing (NLP).

Natural language processing is the task of enabling computers to understand and generate human language. Deep learning models have greatly improved the performance of NLP systems, making them more accurate at tasks such as speech recognition, translation, sentiment analysis, and text summarization.

For instance, deep learning is used in virtual assistants like Siri or Alexa, allowing them to understand spoken commands and respond in a human-like manner.

3. Autonomous Vehicles.

Neural networks and deep learning are at the heart of autonomous vehicle technology. These systems use deep learning models to process data from sensors, cameras, and radars to make real-time decisions about navigation, obstacle avoidance, and path planning. Autonomous vehicles must be able to understand their environment and react appropriately to ensure safety, and deep learning is a key component in achieving this level of intelligence.

4. Healthcare and Medical Imaging.

In the healthcare industry, deep learning models are used to analyze medical images, such as X-rays, MRIs, and CT scans. These models can detect early signs of diseases like cancer, helping doctors make more accurate diagnoses and treatment decisions. Deep learning is also used in drug discovery, where it can help identify potential compounds for new medications.

5. Game Playing.

Deep learning has made significant strides in the world of gaming, where it is used to train AI agents to play complex games like chess, Go, and video games. For example, AlphaGo, an AI developed by DeepMind, used deep learning techniques to defeat human world champions in the game of Go. These AI systems learn to play by simulating thousands or even millions of games, improving their strategies with each iteration.

The Power of Neural Networks and Deep Learning.

The power of neural networks and deep learning lies in their ability to learn complex patterns from large datasets. They can handle unstructured data, such as images and text, and make highly accurate predictions or decisions based on that data. The more data they are trained on, the better they become at solving problems.

These technologies have opened up new possibilities for intelligent systems, enabling them to perform tasks that were once thought to be exclusive to humans. As neural networks and deep learning continue to evolve, their impact on various industries and fields will only grow, leading to even more innovative applications in the future.

By understanding neural networks and deep learning, we gain insight into how intelligent systems are built and how they can be used to solve complex problems. These foundational concepts are crucial for anyone looking to develop intelligent systems, whether for research, business, or other applications.

Chapter 3: Building AI Models from Scratch.

3.1 Data Collection and Preprocessing.

Building a successful artificial intelligence (AI) model begins with the collection of quality data. This is one of the most important steps in the entire process, as the performance of your model heavily depends on the data it is trained on. Data collection and preprocessing lay the foundation for any machine learning task. Without proper data, even the best algorithms will struggle to produce meaningful results.

Data collection involves gathering the information needed to train the AI system, while preprocessing involves cleaning and organizing this data so it can be used effectively. These steps are essential because raw data is often messy, incomplete, or not in a format that can be used directly. In this section, we will discuss the key elements of data collection and preprocessing and how they contribute to the success of AI models.

Understanding the Importance of Data Collection.

In any AI project, the quality and quantity of data play a crucial role. Good data collection starts with a clear understanding of the problem you want the AI model to solve. This understanding will guide you in determining what kind of data is needed. For example, if you want to create a model that predicts house prices, you will need data on factors like square footage, location, number of bedrooms, and more.

There are several sources from which you can collect data:

1. **Public Datasets**: Many industries and organizations provide publicly available datasets that you can use. These datasets often come with a predefined structure, which makes it easier to get started. For example, Kaggle is a popular platform where you can find datasets for different types of AI projects, from image recognition to natural language processing.

2. **Web Scraping**: Sometimes, the data you need is not readily available in a structured

format. In such cases, web scraping can be a useful tool. Web scraping involves extracting data from websites. However, it's important to consider the legal and ethical implications before collecting data in this way.

3. Surveys and Forms: For projects that require more specific or custom data, creating surveys or forms to collect information directly from users can be an effective method. This approach is common in applications where user behavior or preferences are important, such as recommendation systems.

4. Sensors and IoT Devices: In some cases, you may collect data through sensors or other connected devices. This is often seen in projects related to the Internet of Things (IoT), where data from sensors is used to monitor or predict certain behaviors.

5. Existing Company Data: If you are working on a project within a company, existing business data can be a valuable source. Sales data, customer feedback, or operational data might provide the insights needed to train an AI model.

It is important to gather a variety of data points and ensure that they are representative of the problem you want to solve. Data from a single source or time period may not accurately reflect the real-world situation and could lead to biased or unreliable results.

The Role of Data Preprocessing.

Once you've gathered the data, the next critical step is data preprocessing. Raw data is often unclean, noisy, and incomplete. Preprocessing helps convert the data into a usable form by removing errors, filling in missing values, and transforming the data to ensure consistency. Here are the key steps involved in data preprocessing:

1. Handling Missing Data.

One of the most common issues with raw data is the presence of missing values. Incomplete records can occur for many reasons: users may skip questions in a survey, sensors may malfunction, or data may be missing due to system errors.

There are several strategies to deal with missing data:

Imputation: This involves filling in the missing data with estimated values. One common method is to fill missing values with the mean, median, or mode of the available data. In more advanced cases, imputation methods like K-Nearest Neighbors (KNN) or regression imputation can be used to predict the missing values based on existing data.

Deletion: In some cases, rows or columns with missing values can be removed entirely. However, this method should be used with caution, especially if a significant portion of the data is missing.

Flagging: Sometimes, it might be helpful to keep the missing data as a separate category and use a flag to indicate that data is missing. This approach can be useful in situations where the absence of data carries meaning.

2. Data Normalization and Scaling.

Another important preprocessing step is data normalization or scaling. Many AI models, particularly those that involve distance calculations (such as k-nearest neighbors or support vector machines), require that the data be on a similar scale. This is because features with larger numerical ranges could dominate the model's predictions if not scaled appropriately.

For example, if one feature is measured in thousands and another in tens, the feature measured in thousands will have a disproportionate effect on the model. Normalizing or scaling the data ensures that all features contribute equally to the model's performance.

There are several methods for scaling data:

Min-Max Scaling: This method scales the data to a fixed range, typically between 0 and 1. It is done by subtracting the minimum value of a feature and then dividing by the range of the feature.

Standardization (Z-Score Normalization):
This method involves rescaling the data so that
it has a mean of 0 and a standard deviation of
1. This is done by subtracting the mean of the
feature and dividing by the standard deviation.

3. Handling Categorical Data.

In real-world datasets, many features are
categorical, meaning they reflect discrete
categories, such as "yes" or "no" or "red,"
"blue," and "green." These types of features
cannot be directly employed by machine
learning models, which normally require
numerical data.

There are two main ways for translating
category data into numerical form:

One-Hot Encoding: This approach creates a
binary column for each category. For example,
if a feature has three possible categories (red,
blue, and green), one-hot encoding will create
three columns (red, blue, and green), with a 1
indicating the presence of that category and a 0
for the others.

Label Encoding: This approach assigns a
unique integer value to each category. For

example, "red" might be encoded as 0, "blue" as 1, and "green" as 2. While label encoding is simpler, it can sometimes introduce an unwanted ordinal relationship between categories (i.e., red < blue < green), which may not be appropriate for all datasets.

4. Dealing with Outliers.

Outliers are extraordinary values that differ greatly from the remainder of the data. These numbers can affect the output of an AI model, particularly if the model is sensitive to substantial changes in the data.

There are numerous approaches to address outliers:

Removing Outliers: If the outliers are rare and appear to be errors, it might be prudent to eliminate them. However, this selection should be taken cautiously, as outliers could represent genuine data points in certain instances.

Capping: In some circumstances, outliers can be capped to a specific value. This entails setting a threshold for the data so values above or below that threshold are adjusted to the threshold.

5. Feature Engineering.

Feature engineering is the process of selecting, changing, or inventing new features that improve the performance of a machine learning model. This phase is crucial for boosting model accuracy, especially if the raw data doesn't exactly match the relationships you are trying to predict.

Feature engineering can involve:

Creating New Features: Combining multiple features to generate new ones that better reflect the underlying patterns in the data.

Selecting Important Features: Sometimes, not all features are necessary for a model. Selecting the most relevant elements can help decrease noise and enhance performance.

Transforming Features: Applying mathematical operations, like logarithms or polynomials, to transform data in a way that makes it more usable for the model.

The Importance of Quality Data.

Throughout this process, it's vital to note that the quality of the data will directly influence the accuracy and effectiveness of your AI model. Gathering clean, relevant, and sufficient data is vital. A well-preprocessed dataset can make a big difference in how well the model learns from the input and performs on unseen data.

By taking the effort to properly collect and preprocess your data, you ensure that the AI model is trained on the finest possible foundation, setting the way for excellent results. While data preparation might be time-consuming, it is a crucial step that cannot be disregarded. Properly prepared data allows the AI model to learn more effectively and make more accurate predictions in the future.

3.2 Training and Evaluating AI Models.

Once the data has been collected, preprocessed, and is ready for use, it is time to move on to one of the most critical processes in constructing an AI model: training and assessing it. These techniques will help you construct a model that can make correct predictions or classifications depending on the data it is provided.

Training and assessment are key components of the machine learning workflow. The training phase involves teaching the model to recognize patterns in the data, while assessment analyzes how well the model performs once it has been trained. Understanding these processes is critical for ensuring that the model you construct will perform effectively and fit the needs of the task you are working on.

1. Understanding the Training Process.

The first element of constructing an AI model is training it. This entails providing the model with data and changing its internal parameters to reduce the error between its predictions and the actual values. During training, the model learns to map input data to the correct outputs. The process is iterative, meaning the model continues to improve as it processes new data.

Training an AI model typically follows these steps:

Input Data: The model receives input data, which may be in the form of photos, text, numbers, or other sorts of information. Each example in the training data will include both an input and an expected outcome (also called a label). For example, if you are constructing a model to recognize photographs of cats, the input would be an image, and the intended output would be the label "cat."

Model Structure: The model used for training will have a structure that allows it to learn from data. This structure can change based on the challenge and the type of model being employed. For example, in a neural network, the model comprises layers of neurons, each with weights that affect how inputs are translated into outputs. During training, these weights are modified to improve predictions.

Learning: The model learns by modifying its parameters in a way that minimizes the discrepancy between its predictions and the actual outputs. The process of learning entails computing the error, known as the loss, and utilizing that error to alter the model's weights. This approach is continued until the model's performance reaches an acceptable level.

Optimization techniques: Optimization techniques, such as gradient descent, play a significant role in altering the model's weights during training. These techniques assist the model in locating the best settings that reduce the error. Without optimization methods, the model would not be able to properly learn from the data.

2. Overfitting and Underfitting.

During the training process, there are two typical difficulties that may arise: overfitting and underfitting. These flaws can influence the model's capacity to generalize well to new, unseen data.

Overfitting: Overfitting occurs when the model learns the intricacies and noise of the training data to an extent that it negatively affects its performance on new data. Essentially, the model becomes overly specialized to the training set and cannot generalize well to new datasets. To prevent overfitting, approaches such as regularization, cross-validation, or using extra data might be applied.

Underfitting: Underfitting happens when the model is too simplistic to capture the underlying patterns in the data. It fails to learn the links between the input and output adequately. In this situation, the model's predictions will be poor because it is not complex enough to describe the data's structure. To remedy underfitting, you can consider adopting a more sophisticated model, modifying the characteristics utilized for training, or increasing the training time.

The key to training a good model is to achieve the correct balance between overfitting and underfitting. This requires fine-tuning the model's parameters and often necessitates running the model through numerous iterations to determine the ideal configuration.

3. Model Evaluation.

Once the model has been trained, it is time to evaluate how well it works. This step helps you understand the strengths and weaknesses of the model and whether it is suitable for usage in real-world applications. Evaluation often requires testing the model on data it has not seen previously, known as the test data. The purpose is to determine how well the model can generalize to new, unseen data.

There are numerous measures used to evaluate AI models, depending on the goal and the type of model being employed. These metrics provide quantifiable measures of the model's accuracy and reliability. Here are some popular evaluation metrics:

Accuracy: Accuracy is the most fundamental evaluation metric and measures the percentage of true predictions provided by the model. For classification tasks, accuracy is calculated by dividing the number of correct guesses by the total number of predictions. While accuracy is easy, it may not always be the ideal statistic, especially when the data is uneven.

Precision and Recall: Precision and recall are more detailed measures used in instances where accuracy alone may not provide a complete picture. Precision represents the proportion of positive predictions that are actually right, whereas recall indicates the proportion of actual positive cases that the model properly detected. These metrics are particularly useful in circumstances of imbalanced data, where one class is substantially more frequent than the other.

F1 Score: The F1 score combines both precision and recall into a single value by computing their harmonic mean. It is useful when you want to balance both metrics and take into account the trade-off between precision and recall.

Mean Squared Error (MSE): For regression tasks, where the goal is to predict a continuous variable, the mean squared error is widely utilized. It measures the average squared difference between the expected and actual values. A lower MSE shows that the model's predictions are closer to the true values.

Confusion Matrix: A confusion matrix is a table used for classification problems that provides a more detailed perspective of a model's performance. It gives the amount of true positives, false positives, true negatives, and false negatives, which can assist in analyzing how well the model is performing on each class.

The evaluation step gives you insight into the model's effectiveness and whether further improvements are needed. In some circumstances, the model might need to be retrained, or you may need to alter the data preprocessing or model structure to improve performance.

4. Cross-Validation.

One key technique in model evaluation is cross-validation. Cross-validation is a method used to examine how effectively a model generalizes to an independent dataset. It includes partitioning the data into various subsets (or folds) and training the model on some of the folds while testing it on the remaining ones. This method is performed numerous times, with each fold acting as the test set once. The findings are then averaged to generate a more credible approximation of the model's performance.

Cross-validation helps to decrease bias in the evaluation process and provides better knowledge of how the model will perform in real-world circumstances. The most popular form of cross-validation is k-fold cross-validation, where the data is separated into k subgroups. For example, in 5-fold cross-validation, the model is trained on 4 of the subsets and tested on the remaining one, and this process is repeated five times.

5. Hyperparameter Tuning.

Training an AI model is not simply about giving data to the algorithm. It also requires altering hyperparameters, which are external configurations that influence how the model is trained. Hyperparameters are defined before the training process begins and are not learned from the data. These include characteristics such as learning rate, batch size, number of layers in a neural network, and the regularization strength.

The appropriate set of hyperparameters can considerably increase the model's performance. Hyperparameter tuning entails carefully exploring different combinations of hyperparameters to obtain the ideal configuration. There are several strategies for hyperparameter adjustment, such as:

Grid Search: Grid search includes defining a grid of hyperparameter values and training the model with every conceivable combination. This can be computationally expensive but is thorough.

Random Search: Random search randomly samples from the hyperparameter space. It is less exhaustive than grid search but can still find good results with fewer computations.

Bayesian Optimization: This is a more advanced strategy that uses probabilistic models to drive the search for optimal hyperparameters, frequently making the search more efficient.

6. Model Improvement.

After analyzing the model, it is typically required to improve its performance. If the model does not perform well, many steps can be taken to boost its accuracy:

More Data: If the model is underperforming, acquiring more data may help enhance its learning abilities. More data can provide a richer set of examples, allowing the model to generate better predictions.

Different Features: Feature engineering plays an essential part in enhancing model performance. Adjusting the characteristics used for training, or introducing new ones, can make a big difference in the model's efficacy.

Ensemble Methods: In some circumstances, utilizing numerous models in conjunction can increase performance. Ensemble approaches, such as bagging or boosting, integrate the predictions of numerous models to give a more robust outcome.

Training and testing an AI model is a dynamic process that demands attention to detail and thorough analysis of the numerous methodologies and methods available. By following these procedures and consistently refining the model, you may construct a system that gives relevant insights and accurate forecasts.

3.3 Debugging and Optimizing Performance.

Building an AI model is an interesting and challenging adventure, but it doesn't stop once the initial version is generated. After designing the model and validating its fundamental capabilities, the following stage is to confirm that it operates correctly and efficiently. Debugging and optimizing performance are essential components of the process. These actions can considerably increase the quality and efficacy of your model.

1. Understanding the Importance of Debugging.

Debugging is the process of detecting and repairing faults or bugs in the AI model. These problems can develop for different reasons, such as faulty data preprocessing, coding mistakes, or unexpected behavior during training. Debugging lets you understand why the model is not operating as planned and allows you to repair the flaws to improve its functionality.

When debugging an AI model, the first step is to understand the problem. Is the model not learning properly? Are the predictions inaccurate? Or is there an issue with the data it's receiving? Once you know what's wrong, you can start targeting the reason.

There are a few common mistakes that you could face during debugging:

Data Issues: If the data is not properly prepared or includes errors, the model will not learn successfully. This could include missing numbers, erroneous labels, or even incompatible data types. Make sure your dataset is clean and confirm that the pretreatment stages are appropriately applied.

Model Architecture Problems: Sometimes, the structure of the model itself could be the cause of the problem. For example, a neural network could have too many layers or an improper activation function, resulting in poor performance. Review the model architecture to ensure it meets the task at hand.

Overfitting or Underfitting: As discussed before, overfitting and underfitting are two prevalent difficulties in AI model building. If the model is overfitting, it indicates it is learning the noise in the training data rather than the underlying patterns. If it's underfitting, it's not learning enough from the data. In all scenarios, debugging may include modifying the model's complexity, such as adding regularization or utilizing other techniques.

Training Data Errors: Sometimes, the model might be correctly implemented, but the data entering into it is not accurate. This could involve flaws in how the data is processed or formatted. It's crucial to confirm that your data is being loaded into the model appropriately and that the labels fit with the characteristics.

Debugging can often be a time-consuming and repeated procedure, but it's an essential step for assuring your model's success. Keeping a systematic approach and being patient can help you find and fix the issues more efficiently.

2. Debugging Techniques for AI Models.

There are numerous ways that can be employed to debug AI models efficiently. Some of these strategies require employing tools, while others rely on a hands-on approach.

Print Statements and Logs: The easiest and most popular technique to debug code is to use print statements or logs to trace the model's progress. By publishing interim results at different phases of the model's evolution, you may see where things go wrong. For instance, you might print the output of the model after each training period to observe if it's improving. This technique is helpful for spotting basic problems, such as improper data entry or unexpected behavior during training.

Unit Testing: Unit testing is an approach where individual components of the model (such as functions or modules) are tested in isolation to ensure they work as intended. By testing each component of the AI model separately, you can detect flaws early and avoid issues from propagating across the system. For example, you might develop tests to confirm that the data preprocessing procedures are performing correctly or that the model's predictions are in the desired range.

Visualizing Data: Sometimes, the easiest method to uncover difficulties is to visualize the data. This is particularly handy when working with image or text-based models. Visualization can help you see if the model is learning patterns appropriately or if the data is being processed effectively. Tools like Matplotlib or Seaborn can assist in visualizing data distributions, training loss, and other essential metrics.

Cross-Validation: Cross-validation is not only beneficial for model evaluation but can also aid in debugging. By doing cross-validation, you can examine how well the model performs on different subsets of the data, letting you detect potential problems like overfitting or bias. Cross-validation can also help evaluate if a certain issue is data-specific or if it's constant across other datasets.

Check Gradients: In deep learning, the gradients are utilized to update the model's parameters. If the gradients are too tiny (vanishing gradients) or too large (exploding gradients), the model will fail to learn. Debugging the gradients can help detect these difficulties. By monitoring the gradients during training, you may evaluate if alterations to the learning rate or model architecture are needed.

Simplify the Model: If the model is overly complex, it may be difficult to spot the issue. One way to debug is to simplify the model and remove unneeded layers or components. By lowering the model's complexity, you can typically determine where the problem lies. Once the simpler version is operating well, you can progressively add complexity back into the model.

Use Debugging Tools: Many programming languages and libraries offer specific debugging tools. For instance, TensorFlow, Keras, and PyTorch offer debugging and profiling tools incorporated into their frameworks. These tools provide real-time feedback on the model's performance and allow you to move through the code to observe how it is functioning. These tools are essential for tracking down performance bottlenecks and finding faults in the code or model.

3. Optimizing Performance

Once the model is free of errors, it's time to devote attention to performance optimization. Optimizing performance requires enhancing the model's speed and accuracy. In AI models, performance is generally measured by how quickly the model creates predictions and how correct those forecasts are.

There are numerous techniques to optimize an AI model's performance:

Hyperparameter Tuning: As discussed previously, hyperparameters are crucial in defining the model's behavior. Adjusting parameters such as learning rate, batch size, or number of epochs can have a major impact on the model's performance. Hyperparameter tweaking entails systematically attempting new values for each parameter and observing how the model's performance changes. Techniques such as grid search or random search can help you locate the optimal set of hyperparameters.

Use Efficient Algorithms: The choice of algorithm can affect the model's performance. Some algorithms are more computationally expensive than others; therefore, selecting an efficient approach can improve both training and prediction timeframes. For example, simpler models like decision trees may train faster than deep neural networks, but they might not achieve the same degree of accuracy. Weighing the trade-off between speed and accuracy is a critical component of optimization.

Model Compression: After training a model, you can realize that it is huge and requires substantial memory or computational capacity to run. Model compression is a technique used to lower the size of the model while preserving its correctness. This can involve approaches like pruning (removing less relevant elements of the model), quantization (lowering the precision of weights), or employing knowledge distillation (training a smaller model to resemble a larger model).

Parallelization and GPU Usage: Many AI models, especially deep learning models, require significant computational capacity. One technique to speed up training and optimization is to employ parallel computing. Modern AI models generally use GPUs (Graphics Processing Units) instead of traditional CPUs (Central Processing Units) since GPUs are intended to perform the large-scale matrix operations required for machine learning. If your model is not employing GPU acceleration, you can consider redesigning your setup to take advantage of these powerful processors.

Batch Size and Learning Rate: One of the simplest ways to optimize performance is to modify the batch size and learning rate. The batch size specifies how many samples are processed at a time, and the learning rate governs how much the model's weights are updated after each batch. Finding the appropriate values for these factors can have a substantial impact on both training speed and accuracy.

Early halting: Early halting is a technique used to prevent overfitting and optimize training time. It entails monitoring the model's performance on a validation set during training. If the model's performance stops improving or starts to worsen, training is discontinued to prevent overfitting. Early halting can save time and money while ensuring the model's performance stays high.

Ensemble Methods: Sometimes, combining numerous models might lead to greater performance than using a single model. This is known as an ensemble method. For example, strategies like bagging or boosting entail training many models and pooling their predictions. By doing so, the ensemble technique can enhance accuracy and make the model more robust.

Optimizing the performance of an AI model needs a combination of techniques and strategies. Each model is unique, and the strategy to optimization will rely on the individual problem, the type of data, and the computational resources available. Debugging and optimizing performance are continual tasks that demand regular attention and adjustment. With time and experience, you may develop a model that not only functions but also performs at its best.

Chapter 4: Implementing Core AI Features.

4.1 Natural Language Processing (NLP) Fundamentals.

Natural Language Processing, or NLP, is an area of artificial intelligence that focuses on the interaction between computers and human languages. The goal of NLP is to enable computers to read, interpret, and generate human language in a way that is valuable. In the simplest terms, NLP helps machines to process and make sense of textual material, which is something humans do readily but computers find tough.

1. What is natural language processing?

Language is important to human interaction. Every day, we communicate through spoken and written words, from simple conversations to complicated academic texts. For machines to aid in these relationships, they must be able to grasp the words we use and the meaning behind them. This is where NLP comes in.

NLP strives to bridge the gap between human communication and machine understanding. It is concerned with how computers can interpret and make sense of language in both its written and spoken forms. The ultimate goal of NLP is to enable machines to perform tasks such as translating languages, answering queries, summarizing material, and even holding conversations.

2. Challenges in NLP.

Working with human language is not a simple assignment for a machine. There are various challenges to overcome, such as:

Ambiguity: Human language is typically ambiguous, meaning that the same word or phrase can have many meanings depending on the situation. For example, the word "bank" might refer to a financial institution or the side of a river. Understanding the meaning requires context, which can be difficult for a machine to discern.

Complexity of Syntax: Sentences in human language can be formed in limitless ways. For instance, the sentence "The cat sat on the mat" has a different structure than "On the mat, the cat sat." Despite the difference in word order, the meaning stays the same. NLP must account for such variances and grasp the structure of phrases.

Idiomatic Expressions: People regularly employ terms that cannot be comprehended by their literal sense. For instance, the phrase "kick the bucket" is a common idiom meaning "to die," but a computer can understand it as actually kicking a bucket, which leads to confusion.

Nuances in Meaning: Humans often communicate with nuance, expressing feelings or tones through words. A simple sentence like "I love this!" can be said with genuine excitement or sarcastically. Determining the sentiment underlying the words requires comprehending not just the words themselves, but also the context and tone in which they are employed.

Despite these hurdles, tremendous progress has been achieved in NLP, and many jobs that were formerly considered difficult for machines to execute are now within reach.

3. Common NLP Tasks.

There are various frequent jobs that fall under the scope of NLP. These tasks can be roughly grouped into comprehending, creating, and manipulating language:

Text Classification: This work requires categorizing text into different classes or labels. For example, in email filtering, an algorithm might categorize an email as "spam" or "not spam." Text classification is often used in sentiment analysis, where the goal is to detect whether a piece of text communicates a positive, negative, or neutral sentiment.

Named Entity Recognition (NER): NER includes identifying important entities inside text, such as names of people, locations, dates, or organizations. For example, in the line "Apple is releasing a new product in New York on March 15," an NER system would identify "Apple" as a corporation, "New York" as a location, and "March 15" as a date.

Part-of-Speech Tagging (POS): This work requires tagging each word in a phrase with its appropriate part of speech, such as noun, verb, adjective, etc. POS tagging helps to comprehend the grammatical structure of a sentence and plays a crucial part in many NLP applications.

Sentiment Analysis: Sentiment analysis involves determining the emotional tone of a piece of text. For example, it can help identify whether a tweet about a product is positive, negative, or neutral. This activity is widely utilized in social media monitoring and consumer feedback analysis.

Language Translation: Language translation systems are possibly the most well-known example of NLP in use. Machine translation technologies like Google Translate automatically transform text from one language to another. While machine translation has improved over the years, difficulties like idiomatic language and cultural nuances still offer substantial hurdles.

Text Summarization: This includes constructing a condensed version of a text that captures its essential themes. Summarization can be extractive, where essential sentences are selected from the original text, or abstractive, where the system develops a new summary using its understanding of the content.

Question Answering: Question answering systems strive to deliver relevant answers to user queries. This could involve answering factual questions like "What is the capital of France?" or more complex queries such as "What are the benefits of exercise for mental health?" Question answering is often used in search engines, customer service chatbots, and virtual assistants like Siri or Alexa.

4. Techniques in NLP.

To manage the intricacies of human language, NLP uses a range of strategies, typically coupled to obtain the best results. Some of these strategies include:

Tokenization: Tokenization is the process of breaking text into smaller parts, called tokens, which could be words, subwords, or characters. For example, the statement "The quick brown fox" would be tokenized into the words ["The", "quick", "brown", "fox"]. Tokenization is often the initial step in many

NLP jobs and is necessary for preparing text before it can be evaluated.

Stemming and Lemmatization: Stemming and lemmatization are procedures used to reduce words to their base form. For example, "running," "ran," and "runner" might all be reduced to the root word "run." While stemming eliminates suffixes to get to the root, lemmatization is more advanced and uses linguistic information to determine the right base form of a word.

Vectorization: Computers cannot understand language in its raw form. To enable machines to process words, the text must be turned into numbers. This is where vectorization comes in. Common methods of vectorization include Bag-of-Words (BoW), Term Frequency-Inverse Document Frequency (TF-IDF), and Word Embeddings (like Word2Vec or GloVe). These algorithms portray words as vectors, or multidimensional points that capture semantic correlations between words.

Deep Learning Models: Recent advancements in NLP have been fueled by deep learning approaches. Recurrent Neural Networks (RNNs), Long Short-Term Memory (LSTM) networks, and Transformer models like BERT and GPT have considerably increased the ability of machines to interpret and generate language. These models use layers of artificial neurons to interpret language data and learn patterns in the text.

Attention Mechanism: The attention mechanism is a technique used in deep learning models to focus on specific areas of the input when making predictions. In the case of NLP, it helps the model to pay attention to certain words or phrases in a sentence that are more relevant for comprehending the meaning. This is very beneficial in activities like translation or text production.

5. Applications of NLP.

NLP has a wide range of applications that are already making a huge impact in numerous industries. Here are a few examples:

Customer Service Chatbots: Many firms utilize chatbots powered by NLP to assist consumers. These chatbots can answer queries, resolve difficulties, and deliver information, offering 24/7 service. They often utilize sentiment analysis to assess the tone of the customer's communication and respond appropriately.

Search Engines: Search engines like Google rely significantly on NLP to interpret the content of web pages and give relevant search results. NLP techniques such as query understanding and entity recognition assist search engines in matching user searches with the most applicable information.

Voice Assistants: Virtual assistants like Amazon's Alexa, Apple's Siri, and Google Assistant employ NLP to process spoken language and carry out tasks. These assistants rely on speech recognition to transcribe spoken words into text and then utilize NLP to interpret the user's intent.

Social Media Monitoring: Social media platforms and corporations regularly utilize NLP to monitor postings, tweets, and comments. Sentiment analysis helps them understand public opinion regarding products, services, or events. NLP may also recognize trends, identify client complaints, and measure brand reputation.

Healthcare: In the healthcare industry, NLP is used to process and extract information from medical records, enabling doctors and researchers to obtain insights from enormous volumes of unstructured text. NLP can also assist in designing systems that help doctors identify illnesses or prescribe therapies based on patient information.

Content Generation: NLP can also be used to automatically generate text, such as articles, summaries, and reports. Tools like GPT-3 can generate articles that sound like they were written by people, letting businesses publish content at scale.

6. The Future of NLP.

NLP is always changing, with new developments and discoveries coming often. The application of deep learning models, especially transformer-based models, has led to considerable gains in NLP tasks. As computer power increases and new methodologies are developed, the accuracy and efficiency of NLP systems will continue to improve.

Furthermore, as NLP becomes more advanced, it will be able to handle more complicated and subtle language problems. The objective is to construct models that not only understand words and sentences but also grasp the deeper meaning and context behind human communication. This could lead to more human-like interactions with machines and an even larger range of applications across different industries.

4.2 Computer Vision Applications.

Computer vision is an area of artificial intelligence that enables computers to comprehend and make judgments based on visual data, much like how humans use their eyes and brains to perceive the world around them. By processing photos, videos, and other visual data, computer vision systems can identify objects, recognize patterns, and even make predictions. The ultimate goal of computer vision is to enable machines to "see" and interpret the visual world in a way that is beneficial for diverse tasks.

1. What is computer vision?

At its foundation, computer vision tries to empower machines to interpret and understand images and videos, enabling them to do activities that traditionally require human visual awareness. This technology helps computers to filter and evaluate visual data, typically utilizing the same techniques humans use to detect objects, people, and scenes.

Computer vision encompasses a collection of algorithms, models, and approaches that can detect patterns, objects, and other relevant information from raw visual input. The visual data can come from sources like cameras, video recordings, satellite photography, or medical scans.

There are two basic tasks that computer vision focuses on: comprehending the content of an image or video (i.e., what is represented) and making judgments or performing actions based on that content. This includes recognizing items, classifying photos, detecting faces, and even analyzing movements in films.

2. How Does Computer Vision Work?

Computer vision systems generally follow a process of gathering, analyzing, and interpreting visual data. This involves numerous steps:

Image Acquisition: The initial stage in computer vision is getting the visual data, which commonly comes in the form of photos or videos taken by a camera. This data is then translated into a format that the computer can process.

Preprocessing: The raw visual data is often noisy or incomplete; thus, preprocessing is employed to increase its quality. This phase may involve changing the brightness or contrast, reducing noise, or shrinking the image to make it easier for the machine to evaluate.

Feature Extraction: In this step, the computer system detects essential features in the image that help it grasp its content. These qualities could be edges, textures, colors, or shapes that are crucial to distinguishing items or patterns in the image.

Modeling and Recognition: After features are retrieved, the system employs trained models to recognize patterns and generate predictions about what is displayed in the image. This step generally incorporates machine learning algorithms that have been trained on big datasets to understand distinct visual concepts.

Post-processing and Decision Making: Once the system has analyzed the visual data, it may make decisions based on what it has recognized. For example, if the computer vision system sees a cat in an image, it might label the image as "cat" or "pet" and take action, like presenting information on the cat or triggering an alert.

3. Common Applications of Computer Vision.

Computer vision offers a wide range of applications that serve numerous sectors. Below are some of the most common and impactful applications:

Object Detection and Recognition: One of the most common uses of computer vision is object detection, where the system identifies and locates items inside an image. For example, a self-driving car relies on object detection to distinguish pedestrians, other vehicles, road signs, and barriers. Similarly, security systems use object detection to identify intruders or suspect activity.

Face Recognition: Face recognition technology has become one of the most prominent uses of computer vision. This technology can evaluate and identify human faces from photos or video footage. It is utilized in a variety of scenarios, such as unlocking smartphones, safeguarding buildings, or monitoring attendance at events. The method works by detecting key facial traits and comparing them to known faces in a database.

Image Classification: Image classification is a task where the computer vision system assigns a label to an image based on its content. For example, an image classification model can categorize photographs into distinct classifications such as "dog," "cat," or "car." This application is utilized in several domains, such as managing photo libraries, categorizing medical images, or even classifying product images in e-commerce platforms.

Medical Image Analysis: In healthcare, computer vision has shown to be a valuable tool for interpreting medical images. For instance, algorithms can assist clinicians in examining X-rays, MRI scans, or CT scans to find anomalies such as tumors, fractures, or illnesses. Medical image analysis can boost early diagnosis, improve accuracy, and reduce the effort for healthcare personnel.

Autonomous Vehicles: Self-driving automobiles rely largely on computer vision to interpret their environment. These vehicles employ cameras and sensors to record data about their environment, which is subsequently processed by computer vision systems to detect objects, lanes, pedestrians, and traffic signs. This lets the vehicle make safe and educated driving decisions without human interference.

Gesture Recognition: Gesture recognition involves utilizing computer vision to identify human gestures, such as hand movements or facial expressions. This use is particularly beneficial in human-computer interaction, where users can control equipment or communicate with systems using gestures. For example, virtual reality (VR) systems rely on gesture recognition to track user motions and give an immersive experience.

Augmented Reality (AR): In augmented reality, computer vision helps overlay digital information over the real world. By identifying items or landmarks in the surroundings, computer vision helps AR systems to arrange virtual things in a way that appears realistic. This is employed for different purposes, from entertainment and gaming to home design and teaching.

Surveillance and Security: Security systems, such as surveillance cameras, employ computer vision to monitor areas for anomalous activity. These systems can identify intruders, recognize faces, and even follow movements across numerous cameras. By evaluating video footage in real-time, computer vision can provide quick alerts to security personnel, enabling them to respond to events faster.

Retail and Inventory Management: Computer vision is also utilized in the retail business to track inventory, scan products, and aid with checkout processes. For instance, automated checkout systems use computer vision to recognize and process items without the need for manual barcode scanning. Additionally, cameras can monitor shelves and inform store management when stock levels are low.

Agriculture and Farming: In agriculture, computer vision is employed to monitor crops, identify pests, and analyze plant health. By analyzing photos acquired by drones or ground-based cameras, farmers can discover concerns such as infections or nutrient deficits early, allowing for quicker responses. This leads to higher crop yields and more efficient farming practices.

4. Techniques in Computer Vision.

To perform these tasks effectively, computer vision uses a variety of techniques, including:

Image Segmentation: Image segmentation is the process of dividing an image into smaller, meaningful parts. By dividing multiple parts of an image, computer vision systems can focus on specific areas of interest, such as an object or backdrop. Segmentation assists with tasks like object detection, scene interpretation, and medical picture analysis.

Convolutional Neural Networks (CNNs): CNNs are a sort of deep learning algorithm that has changed computer vision. They are particularly well-suited for image identification jobs since they can automatically learn to detect essential elements in images. CNNs consist of numerous layers of convolutional operations, which allow the network to learn hierarchical patterns in images, from simple edges to complicated structures.

Optical Flow: Optical flow refers to the pattern of motion of objects inside a video sequence. By evaluating the movement of pixels between consecutive frames, computer vision systems can track objects and estimate their speed and direction. This approach is commonly utilized in applications like video surveillance, robotics, and autonomous driving.

Object Tracking: Object tracking is a task where the system continuously follows a specific object across a video sequence. This is useful for applications such as security surveillance, when you need to monitor a certain person or object over time. Algorithms can track objects by recognizing essential features and updating their positions as they move inside the frame.

3D Vision: While standard computer vision focuses on 2D images, 3D vision involves understanding and analyzing three-dimensional data. This is especially relevant for applications like robotics and augmented reality, where an awareness of depth and spatial relationships is essential. Techniques such as stereoscopic vision and depth sensors assist in constructing 3D models from 2D photos.

5. Challenges in Computer Vision.

While computer vision has made great progress, there are still difficulties that need to be solved. Some of the common issues in computer vision include:

Variability in Lighting and Viewpoint: Images can vary substantially depending on lighting conditions and the angle from which they are recorded. A face may look different under bright sunlight versus dim light, or an object could appear deformed from different camera angles. Computer vision systems must be robust enough to handle these variances and yet reliably identify things.

Occlusion: In some conditions, things may be partially concealed or hidden by other objects, making them harder to perceive. For example, a person might be standing behind a tree, and parts of their body may not be visible. Computer vision systems must be able to distinguish objects even when they are not fully visible.

Real-time Processing: Many computer vision applications, such as self-driving cars and surveillance systems, require real-time processing of visual data. This means that the system must assess and respond to images or videos instantaneously, which might be computationally expensive. Optimizing computer vision systems to perform efficiently in real-time is a continuous challenge.

Generalization: Machine learning models used in computer vision often function well on the data they were trained on but might struggle with unseen or novel data. For instance, an object detection model trained on a dataset of cats and dogs may not perform well when it encounters a new animal, like a horse. Generalizing to new, unknown data remains a significant difficulty in computer vision.

6. The Future of Computer Vision.

The future of computer vision seems optimistic, with developments in deep learning, 3D imagery, and computational power leading to more accurate and complex systems. As more data becomes available and processing power improves, computer vision will continue to improve, creating new possibilities for industries like healthcare, retail, transportation, and entertainment.

As we continue to create new technologies, the goal is to make computer vision systems more adaptive, robust, and efficient. The future promises enormous potential for computer vision, with applications that could profoundly change the way we live and interact with technology.

Chapter 5:

Integrating AI into Real-World Applications.

5.1 AI in Web and Mobile Applications.

The integration of artificial intelligence (AI) into online and mobile applications has altered how we engage with technology. It has made our lives easier, more efficient, and more individualized. From the apps we use every day to the websites we visit, AI has become a critical component in developing smarter, more intuitive experiences.

1. What is AI in Web and Mobile Applications?

AI in online and mobile applications refers to the use of machine learning, natural language processing, computer vision, and other AI techniques to enhance the operation of these apps. These apps can execute activities such as evaluating user data, making predictions, automating procedures, and creating tailored experiences. By incorporating AI into online and mobile platforms, developers may create more interactive and engaging apps that suit the demands of consumers in ways that were not feasible previously.

For example, many mobile apps currently use AI to understand and anticipate user behavior. A music streaming app can recommend songs based on the user's listening history, while a fitness app can track progress and offer recommendations customized to the user's health goals. Similarly, AI in online apps can enable chatbots that assist customers with routine inquiries or provide customer service, making interactions quicker and more efficient.

2. The Role of AI in Web Applications.

AI is transforming the way we engage with websites. Many businesses and organizations employ AI-powered features to boost customer engagement and create personalized experiences. Here are a few instances of how AI is being applied in online applications:

Personalized Content: One of the most prevalent applications of AI in web apps is content personalization. Websites utilize AI to track user activity and analyze their preferences to present material that is relevant to them. For example, e-commerce companies utilize AI to recommend products based on past browsing or purchase activity. News websites might propose stories based on a user's reading history or interests.

Chatbots and Virtual Assistants: Many websites now incorporate AI-powered chatbots and virtual assistants that help users discover information, answer queries, or complete activities. These tools can aid with everything from debugging issues on an e-commerce site to helping users traverse complex web platforms. Chatbots can handle simple inquiries, while more powerful systems can manage complicated jobs, delivering quick customer service and decreasing the need for human participation.

Search Engine Optimization (SEO): AI plays a role in search engine optimization by helping websites enhance their ranks. Through approaches such as keyword analysis and content optimization, AI can ensure that a website shows in relevant search results. Some AI systems even assist websites in forecasting what people might be searching for, enhancing search results and driving content creation.

Data Analysis and Insights: AI-driven data analysis tools are vital for analyzing user activity on websites. They can discover trends and patterns in how consumers interact with content, helping businesses optimize their websites for greater engagement and conversion rates. For example, AI can assess how users traverse a site, what pages they visit the most, and where they tend to leave off, providing significant data for website optimization.

Fraud Detection: AI is increasingly being employed in web apps for security objectives. By examining patterns of user behavior, AI systems can spot potential fraud or criminal activities on a website. For instance, e-commerce platforms utilize AI to detect anomalous activities, helping to protect consumers' financial information and maintain secure transactions.

3. The Role of AI in Mobile Applications.

Mobile applications are arguably even more reliant on AI than web applications. Given the strong relationship people have with their smartphones, the incorporation of AI in mobile apps offers various benefits. Mobile devices provide ample options for collecting user data, making them perfect for applications that demand real-time processing and personalized experiences. Here are some ways in which AI is strengthening mobile applications:

Personalized User Experience: One of the most powerful uses of AI in mobile apps is personalization. Mobile apps employ AI to understand users' preferences and habits, changing the app experience accordingly. For instance, social networking apps evaluate your interactions, such as likes, shares, and comments, to select material that corresponds with your preferences. Similarly, fitness apps analyze your activity and progress, delivering individualized training regimens and nutrition suggestions depending on your goals.

Voice Assistants: Voice-controlled programs, such as Siri, Google Assistant, and Alexa, rely significantly on AI to interpret and respond to user commands. These virtual assistants employ natural language processing (NLP) to understand spoken language and respond intelligently. They may create reminders, answer queries, manage smart home devices, and conduct numerous other functions, giving a hands-free experience for consumers.

Picture Recognition and Augmented Reality (AR): Mobile applications increasingly leverage AI-powered picture recognition and augmented reality to create unique user experiences. For example, social media platforms like Instagram and Snapchat employ AI to recognize faces and objects in images, giving capabilities such as automated tagging and filters. Shopping apps use AR to allow consumers to imagine how furniture or apparel will look in their home before making a purchase. These features make the mobile experience more interactive and engaging.

Predictive Text and Autocorrect: Predictive text and autocorrect functionalities in messaging and typing apps are powered by AI. These features learn from users' historical typing habits and preferences, boosting the accuracy of predictions and helping users type quicker. As you type, the app guesses the next word or proposes adjustments, making communication more efficient.

Health and Fitness Tracking: Many mobile health and fitness apps employ AI to track users' health and deliver individualized suggestions. These apps can track physical activity, sleep habits, heart rate, and other vital signs, delivering information that might help users lead healthier lifestyles. For instance, AI can offer individualized training regimens or diet plans based on data acquired from the user's behaviors and interests.

Photo and Video Editing: AI is also making its way into photo and video editing apps. Features such as automatic image improvement, background removal, and object detection are powered by AI algorithms. These apps allow users to generate professional-looking photographs and movies without needing expert editing abilities, making creative tools more accessible to everyone.

4. Benefits of AI in Web and Mobile Applications.

Integrating AI into online and mobile applications offers a wide range of benefits for both consumers and developers. For users, AI boosts convenience, customization, and overall user experience. For developers and organizations, AI gives vital insights into user behavior and preferences, improving engagement and raising conversion rates.

Improved User Experience: By personalizing content and interactions, AI makes apps and websites more fun to use. Users are more likely to stay connected with an app or website that gives personalized recommendations and services tailored to their needs.

Increased Efficiency: AI-powered automation, such as chatbots and voice assistants, helps streamline activities and boost efficiency. Users can get rapid answers or support without waiting for a person representative, making interactions faster and more convenient.

Better Decision-Making: For businesses, AI can evaluate enormous volumes of data and deliver insights that drive better decision-making. Whether it's altering marketing strategy, optimizing content, or increasing customer care, AI helps businesses make smart choices that lead to success.

Scalability: AI systems can help apps scale more efficiently. As user numbers expand, AI can handle an increasing amount of data, ensuring that the app continues to work effectively without requiring enormous manual involvement.

Cost-Effective Solutions: AI can cut expenses by automating repetitive jobs and processes. For instance, chatbots can answer simple customer support requests, freeing up human agents to focus on more difficult issues. In this approach, AI can help firms save on labor costs while enhancing customer happiness.

5. Challenges of AI in Web and Mobile Applications.

While AI offers many benefits, integrating it into online and mobile applications is not without its obstacles. Some of the common obstacles developers confront include:

Data Privacy and Security: Since AI systems rely on large volumes of data to generate accurate predictions, safeguarding the privacy and security of that data is a big concern. Developers must adopt comprehensive security measures to secure users' personal information and comply with data protection requirements.

Cost and Resources: Developing AI-powered applications can be resource-intensive, needing advanced algorithms, high-quality data, and powerful hardware. This can be costly for businesses, especially for startups or small enterprises.

Complexity: AI integration can make an application more complex to design and maintain. Developers need to be knowledgeable in AI technology and ensure that the system functions flawlessly with other components of the app.

Ethical Concerns: As AI becomes more advanced, ethical concerns related to bias, fairness, and transparency arise. Developers must ensure that their AI systems are designed to avoid discrimination and that they operate in a fair and transparent manner.

6. Future of AI in Web and Mobile Applications.

The future of AI in web and mobile applications looks bright. As technology continues to advance, AI-powered features will become even more sophisticated, enabling new forms of personalization, automation, and interactivity. We can expect even more seamless and intuitive user experiences across all types of platforms.

The integration of AI will continue to play a pivotal role in how businesses engage with users and how users interact with digital content. In the coming years, AI will help shape the future of web and mobile applications, leading to smarter, more responsive, and more efficient systems that will benefit both users and businesses alike.

5.2 Automating Workflows with AI Tools.

In today's fast-paced world, automation has become an essential tool for businesses and individuals alike. Artificial intelligence (AI) has played a significant role in transforming how we automate tasks, from simple actions to more complex processes. By automating workflows, organizations can streamline operations, reduce human error, and free up time for employees to focus on more strategic tasks.

AI tools have made it possible to automate workflows across a wide variety of industries. These tools help by handling repetitive tasks, making decisions based on data, and even managing processes in real-time. As technology continues to advance, the possibilities for automating workflows are only growing.

1. What Does Automating Workflows Mean?

Automating workflows involves using technology to complete tasks that were previously done manually. In the past, employees spent a considerable amount of time on repetitive tasks that didn't require creativity or problem-solving. These tasks could range from entering data into a system, scheduling meetings, and processing orders to managing customer support requests. Automation can take over many of these duties, allowing businesses to increase efficiency and reduce costs.

When AI tools are integrated into workflows, they can be used to make intelligent decisions, predict outcomes, and improve the overall speed of tasks. Whether it's sorting through large datasets, answering customer inquiries, or managing communications, AI systems are increasingly capable of performing these tasks faster and more accurately than humans.

2. How AI Tools Automate Repetitive Tasks.

One of the primary advantages of AI in workflow automation is the ability to handle repetitive tasks without the need for human intervention. These tasks may be mundane and time-consuming but are essential to the smooth running of any business. By automating them, businesses can reduce human error and save valuable time. Some of the most common AI tools used for automating repetitive tasks include:

Chatbots: AI-powered chatbots have become a standard tool for automating customer service workflows. Instead than having a human representative to answer simple questions or address fundamental difficulties, chatbots may accomplish these duties automatically. They are programmed to answer frequently asked inquiries, provide customer service, and even coach customers through troubleshooting operations. This reduces the time spent by personnel on these basic operations and ensures that clients get the service they need without delays.

Data Entry and Processing: Many organizations rely on vast amounts of data that need to be processed and input into systems. AI solutions can automate this process by extracting essential information from documents, emails, or forms and entering it into databases. This avoids the need for manual data entry, which is not only time-consuming but also prone to human mistakes.

Email Management: Email inboxes may be burdensome, especially for firms that deal with a significant volume of correspondence. AI solutions can help manage and automate email workflows by sorting messages, identifying critical emails, and even generating responses. For example, AI systems can be trained to prioritize emails from specific contacts or with certain phrases, making it easier to manage inboxes and answer swiftly.

Appointment Scheduling: Scheduling meetings and appointments can often be a burden, especially when working with many parties. AI solutions can help automate this process by reviewing participants' calendars, proposing available times, and issuing calendar invites without the requirement for human interaction. This reduces the back-and-forth sometimes needed in setting up meetings and ensuring that schedules are efficiently maintained.

3. Making Data-Driven Decisions.

Automating workflows using AI is not just about performing mundane activities; it's also about making intelligent judgments based on data. AI can examine enormous datasets to uncover patterns, trends, and insights that might not be immediately evident to humans. This ability to make data-driven decisions has a huge impact on numerous corporate areas, such as marketing, operations, and customer support.

Predictive Analytics: AI solutions can help firms make more informed decisions by giving predictive insights. For example, an AI system might examine sales data to forecast future patterns, enabling firms to anticipate demand and change their strategy accordingly. Similarly, AI systems may forecast customer behavior, indicating which customers are most likely to make a purchase, renew a subscription, or churn. This helps firms to target their efforts more efficiently and devote resources where they're most needed.

Personalization: Many organizations employ AI to offer individualized experiences for their customers. By evaluating data such as purchasing history, browsing behavior, and demographics, AI technologies can offer products, services, or content that are tailored to individual interests. This form of customization can boost customer satisfaction and raise conversion rates, as customers are more inclined to engage with content and products that fit with their interests.

Customer Insights: AI can also be used to assess customer comments and sentiment. Tools that analyze social media, reviews, or direct customer feedback can give organizations significant information into how their products or services are regarded. This information can be utilized to improve offers, handle client issues, and change corporate plans.

4. Integrating AI into Business Operations.

Automating workflows using AI is not merely a matter of leveraging discrete tools or technology. For the full benefit of AI to be achieved, it needs to be integrated into a company's larger operations. When AI solutions are effortlessly blended into existing systems, businesses may build more efficient, productive, and cost-effective workflows.

Supply Chain Automation: AI can automate different parts of supply chain management, from inventory tracking to order fulfillment. For example, AI systems can detect when inventory levels are running low, automatically restock products, and even manage shipment operations. This can help firms maintain a smooth flow of goods, prevent delays, and ensure customers receive their orders on schedule.

Human Resource Management: HR departments are sometimes bogged down by administrative chores such as maintaining staff schedules, processing payroll, and screening job applications. AI solutions can assist in automating these chores, allowing HR people to focus on more strategic operations, such as talent development and employee engagement. AI may also assist in hiring by assessing resumes, performing preliminary interviews, and even screening individuals based on particular criteria.

Financial Automation: AI tools are also revolutionizing the finance and accounting divisions of enterprises. From automating invoice processing to reconciling financial data, AI can undertake many of the duties previously done by human staff. For example, AI systems can indicate anomalies in financial accounts, detect fraud, or predict cash flow challenges based on past data, allowing firms to take proactive steps before problems develop.

Marketing Automation: AI plays a crucial part in marketing automation by enabling firms to deliver personalized content, manage campaigns, and measure effectiveness. AI solutions can segment customers, track interaction, and optimize content delivery, ensuring that marketing messages are provided at the correct moment to the right audience. This boosts the effectiveness of marketing campaigns and helps firms achieve their goals more efficiently.

5. Improving Efficiency with AI Workflow Automation.

By automating procedures with AI tools, firms can drastically boost efficiency and productivity. Instead of wasting time on manual operations, staff may focus on jobs that involve creativity, problem-solving, and strategic thinking. Additionally, AI-powered automation helps reduce the risk of human mistakes, ensuring that jobs are executed precisely and on time.

Reduced operating expenses: Automation can cut operating expenses by reducing the need for additional staff to conduct repetitive tasks. It also decreases the risks of errors, which can be costly to rectify. By depending on AI for these jobs, firms can save money and deploy resources more effectively.

Faster Task Completion: One of the most immediate benefits of AI-driven workflow automation is the speed at which activities may be performed. For example, AI can process data, sort through emails, or prepare reports in a fraction of the time it would take a human. This allows organizations to speed up their operations and respond to market developments or client wants more swiftly.

Scalability: As organizations grow, so do their workflows. AI technologies are extremely scalable, meaning they can manage rising volumes of work without affecting efficiency or speed. Whether it's processing more data, managing greater customer contacts, or handling larger inventories, AI systems can expand with a business's needs.

6. Challenges of Automating Workflows Using AI.

While the benefits of process automation using AI are evident, there are also certain limitations that firms must address. Integrating AI technologies into existing workflows can be challenging, and there may be technical, financial, and operational challenges to overcome.

Technical Challenges: Implementing AI technologies into workflows requires technical skills, and the integration process might be challenging. Businesses need to guarantee that the AI systems are compatible with their existing infrastructure and that they perform as intended. This may take substantial time and effort in designing specialized solutions.

Cost of Implementation: While AI can save money in the long term, the initial cost of installing AI technologies can be considerable. Businesses need to invest in the correct technology, software, and skills, which may involve a considerable upfront expenditure. Additionally, organizations must guarantee that the benefits of automation justify these expenditures.

Data Privacy and Security: Since AI systems rely on data, firms must guarantee that they are complying with data privacy standards. Protecting sensitive customer information and ensuring that AI systems operate securely is essential to maintaining customer trust and avoiding potential legal issues.

7. The Future of Workflow Automation with AI.

The future of workflow automation with AI looks promising. As AI technology continues to progress, we may expect even more sophisticated systems that can perform increasingly demanding jobs. Businesses will be able to automate a greater range of activities, producing more efficient and effective workflows.

AI's ability to learn and adapt will also play a vital part in the future of automation. AI systems will get more sophisticated over time, able to make better decisions and forecast outcomes more accurately. This will make process automation not merely a tool for efficiency but a vital engine of business growth and innovation.

As businesses continue to adopt AI and incorporate it into their operations, workflow automation will become a standard practice, helping organizations decrease costs, enhance productivity, and create better experiences for both staff and customers.

5.3 Ethical Considerations in AI Deployment.

As artificial intelligence continues to shape numerous businesses, it carries with it a set of ethical problems that must be handled properly. AI is capable of digesting enormous amounts of data, making judgments, and executing activities that were once only achievable through human participation. While this offers up many possibilities, it also raises concerns about justice, privacy, responsibility, and openness.

Ethical considerations in AI deployment are crucial to guarantee that these technologies are used in a way that benefits society and minimizes harm. As we integrate AI systems into real-world applications, it is crucial to understand the potential consequences and seek to prevent negative outcomes. Let's take a deeper look at some of the significant ethical challenges that occur when AI is used in various sectors.

1. Bias and Fairness in AI Systems.

One of the key ethical challenges in AI is the possibility for bias. AI systems learn from data, and the data they utilize often mirrors historical trends, behaviors, and decisions made by people. If the data is biased in any manner, the AI system can unwittingly learn and perpetuate that bias. This can lead to unequal outcomes, especially in areas like recruiting, financing, law enforcement, and healthcare.

For example, if an AI system is educated on data that shows racial or gender prejudices, it may make conclusions that are unfair or discriminatory. In hiring applications, an AI system might favor one demographic over another based on historical hiring patterns, even if it is not specifically programmed to do so. Similarly, skewed data in the criminal justice system may lead to erroneous projections about an individual's chance of re-offending, potentially leading to harsher sentencing.

To overcome this issue, it is necessary to guarantee that AI systems are trained on diverse and representative datasets. Moreover, regular audits and assessments of the AI system should be done to identify and correct any unexpected biases. Transparency in the design of AI systems and the inclusion of varied opinions during the development process can also assist in preventing bias.

2. Privacy and Data Protection.

As AI systems generally require enormous volumes of personal data to make informed decisions, privacy is a serious ethical challenge. Personal data such as medical records, financial information, internet behavior, and location might be helpful to AI models, but it also raises problems about how that data is acquired, handled, and used.

In many circumstances, individuals may not be entirely aware of how their data is being used or may not have given explicit agreement for it to be used in AI systems. This lack of transparency might destroy trust between consumers and enterprises that adopt AI technology. In some situations, personal data might be exploited or fall into the wrong hands, leading to identity theft, discrimination, or other undesirable results.

To preserve privacy, AI developers must integrate data protection techniques such as anonymization and encryption. They also need to conform to data privacy laws, such as the General Data Protection Regulation (GDPR) in the European Union, which provides individuals full control over their personal data. Ensuring that data is gathered with consent and utilized responsibly is a vital aspect of adopting AI in an ethical manner.

3. Accountability and Transparency.

AI systems frequently operate as "black boxes," meaning their decision-making processes are not necessarily transparent or easily understood by humans. This can create issues when it comes to accountability. If an AI system makes a choice that leads to a negative outcome, such as a mistaken refusal of a loan or an unlawful arrest, it might be difficult to determine who is accountable for the decision. Is it the developer who designed the system, the corporation that installed it, or the AI system itself?

This lack of accountability can damage trust in AI systems and create scenarios where individuals or organizations escape responsibility for the impact of their decisions. Transparency in AI decision-making is vital to guarantee that these technologies are used in a fair and responsible manner.

One method to overcome this is by ensuring that AI models are interpretable and that their decision-making processes can be understood by humans. For example, employing explainable AI (XAI) methodologies can assist in elucidating how an AI system arrives at its findings. Developers should also be honest about the data and algorithms used to train AI models, providing comprehensive explanations of their design choices. This helps ensure that AI systems are not just effective but also ethically sound.

4. Job Displacement and Economic Impact.

AI has the ability to change sectors and generate new opportunities, but it can also lead to job loss. As automation gets more advanced, certain professions that were once handled by humans may become obsolete. For example, AI-powered systems can execute duties in customer service, data input, and even driving, and possibly eliminating individuals in these industries.

The ethical dilemma here is how to combine the benefits of AI with the social obligation of helping workers who may be replaced. In other circumstances, workers may lack the abilities or education to shift to new occupations that need more advanced technical expertise. This could lead to greater income disparity and economic upheaval if not managed appropriately.

To address these concerns, authorities, corporations, and educational institutions must combine to create retraining and reskilling opportunities for workers. This will ensure that people are able to adapt to the changing employment market and take advantage of the new opportunities generated by AI. Additionally, organizations using AI systems should take into account the broader social impact of their technology, working to prevent possible harm to the workforce.

5. Autonomous Systems and Decision-Making.

AI is increasingly being employed in autonomous systems, such as self-driving cars, drones, and robots. These systems are capable of making judgments without human input, which offers distinct ethical challenges. In circumstances when an autonomous system must make a choice that affects human life, such as in the case of a self-driving car deciding how to avoid an accident, ethical difficulties arise.

For example, should an autonomous vehicle prioritize the safety of its passengers, even if it means endangering pedestrians? How should a drone deployed for military purposes make decisions about targeting or engaging with a threat? These actions involve fundamental ethical problems concerning responsibility, fairness, and the value of human life.

In such instances, it is vital to have clear ethical principles and regulatory frameworks in place. Developers of autonomous systems must engage with ethicists, policymakers, and the public to set rules that govern the decision-making processes of these systems. These systems should be programmed to prioritize human safety and well-being and to make decisions in a way that accords with society norms.

6. The Role of Human Judgment in AI Deployment.

While AI systems have the ability to make decisions based on data, there is still a significant role for human judgment in the deployment and management of these systems. AI can assist in decision-making, but it should not replace the requirement for human scrutiny. In many circumstances, human interaction is important to guarantee that AI technologies are used ethically and responsibly.

For example, in healthcare applications, AI can analyze medical data and offer therapies, but healthcare personnel must finally make the final choice. This is especially crucial in complex circumstances when the background, patient preferences, and other considerations may influence the optimal course of action. Relying purely on AI without human judgment could lead to conclusions that do not take into consideration the subtleties of specific situations.

As AI continues to advance, it is crucial to establish a balance between automation and human decision-making. AI should be considered as a tool to support and augment human capabilities, not replace them totally. The ethical deployment of AI demands retaining a human-centered approach, where AI helps human well-being and promotes fairness, rather than replacing human decision-making totally.

7. Long-Term Implications of AI.

As AI becomes more incorporated into numerous areas, we must also examine its long-term ramifications. AI has the potential to transform society in deep ways, from how we work to how we interact with each other. The ethical deployment of AI is not just about addressing existing concerns but also anticipating the obstacles that may come in the future.

For example, AI could significantly transform how we approach education, healthcare, and governance. If not regulated appropriately, AI could lead to increased social inequity, spying, or even the erosion of privacy. It is vital to evaluate these long-term implications and build ethical frameworks that account for the potential risks connected with AI adoption.

Policymakers, industry leaders, and researchers must collaborate to ensure that AI is developed and deployed in a way that aligns with the ideals of fairness, openness, and accountability. As AI continues to grow, we must be attentive in evaluating its influence on society and make modifications as needed to guarantee that its advantages are enjoyed by all.

8. Ethics Beyond the Human Perspective.

Ethical considerations in AI also extend beyond human concerns. As AI systems are being deployed in areas such as environmental monitoring, animal conservation, and climate change management, they must be built to respect the planet and other forms of life. The ethical implications of AI should examine the broader influence on ecosystems, natural resources, and biodiversity.

AI can be a powerful instrument in addressing global concerns, but it is crucial to acknowledge that its deployment should be governed by ethical norms that value the well-being of the earth as well as people.

Chapter 6: Advancing Your AI Skills

6.1 Experimenting with Advanced Architectures.

As you grow in your path of constructing AI models, you may begin to feel ready to tackle increasingly complicated and advanced designs. These are the fundamental blocks underpinning some of the most powerful AI applications today. While earlier stages of AI development frequently involve simpler models, experimenting with sophisticated architectures allows you to design more robust and accurate systems. By working with these advanced frameworks, you may take your talents to the next level, pushing the frontiers of what is possible with artificial intelligence.

Advanced architectures are frequently built to tackle more sophisticated tasks that need higher levels of computational power and deeper understanding of data. From complex neural networks to reinforcement learning models, the realm of AI provides a vast spectrum of possibilities. Let's talk out some of the important architectures you may encounter as you move forward.

1. Deep Neural Networks (DNNs).

Deep neural networks (DNNs) are a form of neural network with numerous layers between the input and output layers. These layers allow the network to learn from data in a more complex way. While standard neural networks could have a few layers, deep networks contain many more, which gives them the potential to simulate more complex relationships.

When dealing with DNNs, you will normally need a substantial amount of data and processing resources. The power of DNNs resides in their capacity to recognize patterns and relationships that could be difficult for humans to detect. For example, they are very useful in picture identification jobs where elements like edges, colors, and textures must be learned by the model.

To experiment with DNNs, you will need to learn how to create and train these deep architectures. This entails selecting the proper number of layers, deciding on activation functions, and choosing an optimizer that helps the model converge to the optimum solution. Advanced architectures sometimes come with increased complexity, but they also provide the possibility for major increases in performance.

2. Convolutional Neural Networks (CNNs).

One of the most important advanced designs you will meet is Convolutional Neural Networks (CNNs). CNNs are designed to analyze grid-like data, such as photographs, and are particularly effective at learning spatial hierarchies in visual data. They excel at spotting patterns, edges, and textures, making them excellent for tasks such as picture classification, object detection, and facial recognition.

In CNNs, convolutional layers are used to scan input data, recognizing low-level characteristics that build up into higher-level representations as the data goes through the network. Pooling layers assist in decreasing the spatial dimensions of the input, allowing the network to focus on the most essential aspects. Fully linked layers at the end of the network combine these features to make the final conclusion or prediction.

Experimenting with CNNs entails working with various configurations of convolutional and pooling layers. You'll need to choose the correct kernel size, stride, and padding to improve the model's performance. Additionally, learning how to prevent overfitting by using techniques like dropout and data augmentation is vital for creating deep convolutional networks.

As you play with CNNs, you'll begin to grasp how different layers interact and how they may be tweaked to achieve high accuracy in image recognition tasks. This type of architecture is employed in a wide range of applications, from self-driving cars to medical picture analysis, and having skill in it can open up numerous prospects in AI research.

3. Recurrent Neural Networks (RNNs).

Another strong architecture you may wish to investigate is Recurrent Neural Networks (RNNs). RNNs are built for sequential data, such as time series or spoken language, and are able to keep an internal state that helps them recall information from earlier inputs. This makes them particularly valuable for applications like speech recognition, language modeling, and sentiment analysis.

In RNNs, each neuron is connected to itself, generating loops that allow the network to process sequences one step at a time. This internal feedback mechanism helps the network maintain context, which is critical when dealing with input that has a temporal or sequential structure.

While traditional RNNs are effective, they can struggle with long-term dependencies because of the vanishing gradient problem. To circumvent this constraint, advanced variants of RNNs, such as Long Short-Term Memory (LSTM) networks and Gated Recurrent Units (GRUs), have been developed. These structures are better suited for learning long-term dependencies, making them excellent for more complex sequential tasks.

Experimenting with RNNs includes learning how to format the data for sequential processing and picking the proper type of

RNN for the task at hand. By working with RNNs, you will learn how to manage time-dependent data and construct systems that can make predictions based on prior occurrences or behaviors.

4. Generative Adversarial Networks (GANs).

Generative Adversarial Networks (GANs) represent one of the most intriguing and novel advancements in AI in recent years. GANs are constructed of two networks: a generator and a discriminator. The generator creates bogus data, such as images or audio, while the discriminator attempts to discern between actual and fake data. The two networks compete in a game, with the generator learning to provide increasingly realistic data and the discriminator learning to better identify phony data.

The beauty of GANs resides in their capacity to generate data that is essentially indistinguishable from genuine data. For example, GANs have been used to generate lifelike photographs of faces, even though the persons in the photos don't exist. They can also be used for data augmentation, boosting the diversity of training data when real data is low.

Working with GANs demands understanding how to balance the training of the generator and discriminator to guarantee that both networks improve simultaneously. This can be hard, as GANs are prone to issues like mode collapse, where the generator produces limited or repeating outputs. However, with the correct methodology, GANs can generate remarkable outcomes in picture production, video synthesis, and creative activities.

Experimenting with GANs includes knowing how to create both the generator and discriminator networks, picking the correct loss functions, and understanding the delicate balance between the two. GANs have multiple applications in domains such as art, entertainment, and research, and having skill in this area might open up many opportunities for AI-driven innovation.

5. Reinforcement Learning (RL).

Reinforcement Learning (RL) is a branch of AI focused on decision-making and control. In RL, an agent learns to make decisions by interacting with an environment and receiving feedback in the form of rewards or penalties. Over time, the agent learns to maximize its cumulative reward, finally learning the best method or policy for attaining its goals.

RL is utilized in a wide range of applications, including robotics, game playing, and autonomous driving. One of the most notable examples of RL in action is AlphaGo, the AI that defeated world champions in the game of Go. By experimenting with RL algorithms, you can develop systems that learn to optimize their behavior in dynamic and complicated contexts.

To explore with RL, you will need to understand concepts such as exploration versus exploitation, reward functions, and the distinction between model-free and model-based techniques. Working with RL also involves an understanding of algorithms like Q-learning and deep Q-networks (DQNs), as well as advanced techniques like policy gradient methods and actor-critic models.

Reinforcement learning offers a unique way of thinking about problem-solving and decision-making, and experimenting with RL will give you vital insights into how autonomous systems may be trained to operate in the real world. While it can be tough, RL is a topic that is quickly evolving and holds considerable promise for future applications.

6. Transformer Architectures.

In recent years, transformer topologies have transformed the field of natural language processing. Transformers use self-attention methods to process incoming data in parallel, allowing them to manage long-range dependencies more successfully than typical RNNs. Transformers have become the foundation for some of the most powerful language models today, such as GPT and BERT.

The self-attention mechanism in transformers allows the model to give varying levels of priority to different areas of the input data, helping it understand the relationships between words or phrases in a sentence. This is particularly beneficial in tasks like machine translation, summarization, and question answering.

When dealing with transformer models, it is crucial to understand how attention mechanisms function and how to fine-tune the model for certain activities. Experimenting with transformers requires working with enormous datasets and employing pre-trained models to fine-tune them for your individual use case. While transformers are computationally expensive, they give remarkable performance in language-related tasks.

Experimenting with sophisticated architectures is an interesting and gratifying element of AI development. As you continue to work with more complicated models, you will acquire deeper insights into how AI systems function and how they may be utilized to tackle a wide range of problems. Each architecture comes with its own set of hurdles and learning curves, but with patience and a commitment to understanding the underlying principles, you will be able to master these sophisticated methodologies and take your AI talents to the next level.

6.2 Scaling AI Systems for Production.

As you continue to build your talents in artificial intelligence, you may eventually confront the difficulty of scaling your AI systems for production situations. While constructing a model is an exciting step, implementing that model at scale involves its own set of obstacles and considerations. You need to ensure that your system functions reliably and efficiently under real-world settings. Scaling AI systems is not just about making models function for a few cases but ensuring that they manage vast volumes of data, operate in dynamic situations, and remain robust in the face of changing inputs.

When it comes to scaling AI systems, there are several crucial things to bear in mind. From physical infrastructure to data pipelines, the decisions you make during the scaling process will directly affect how well your system operates. Let's break down some of the primary procedures and tactics you can use to scale your AI models and make them appropriate for production.

1. Optimizing the Model for Performance.

One of the first steps in scaling an AI system is to optimize the model itself. In a production context, your model must be fast, efficient, and able to manage massive amounts of data. This can need revisions to the model design, the techniques utilized, or even the hardware it operates on.

A major factor is the model's inference time. Inference refers to the process of forming predictions or conclusions based on fresh data. For real-time applications, such as recommendation systems or autonomous vehicles, quick inference is crucial. You will need to fine-tune your model to reduce latency, which can require lowering the complexity of your model, utilizing more efficient algorithms, or applying compression techniques to make the model smaller.

Another part of optimization is ensuring that your model can scale with additional data. As your system handles more input, the model must maintain its performance. You may need to use strategies such as model pruning, where less significant weights or parameters are eliminated, or quantization, which reduces the precision of the model's calculations to speed up processing without compromising too much accuracy.

Optimizing the model for production isn't a one-time operation. It is a continual process. As your system expands and new data becomes available, you will need to regularly analyze and update your model to ensure that it works at its optimum.

2. Distributed Systems for Large-Scale Deployment.

As your AI system scales, you may need to split the burden over numerous servers or workstations. A single server might work fine for small-scale applications, but when the volume of data or the intricacy of the activity increases, you'll need a distributed system.

Distributed systems allow your AI model to handle larger datasets and more demanding computations by sharing the effort among numerous processors. This strategy boosts your system's capacity and enables it to process data more quickly. However, maintaining distributed systems presents its own issues, such as network latency, data consistency, and load balancing.

One prevalent solution for distributed AI tasks is employing cloud computing platforms. These platforms give the required capacity to scale AI applications without the requirement for managing physical servers. With cloud platforms, you can dynamically allocate resources based on the demand, which helps optimize costs and ensure that your system stays responsive even during peak usage times.

There are also specialized technologies that make it easier to scale AI systems in a dispersed scenario. For example, frameworks like Apache Spark or TensorFlow Distributed allow you to partition the training of AI models across numerous nodes, lowering the time needed to train huge models. By using these technologies, you can disperse the data and computations efficiently and ensure that your

AI system can scale seamlessly as demand increases.

3. Data Management and Pipelines.

AI systems rely on massive volumes of data, and one of the most critical components of growing your system is managing that data correctly. Data must be acquired, cleansed, processed, and stored in ways that make it available for AI models to learn from and make predictions.

To scale your AI system, you need a robust data pipeline. A data pipeline is a set of operations that automate the collection, transformation, and storage of data. It is crucial to ensure that your data pipeline is efficient, scalable, and trustworthy, especially as the volume of data increases.

When growing AI systems, you must consider how to handle continuous data streams. For example, in applications such as financial trading, social media monitoring, or IoT devices, data is continually being generated. Your system needs to be able to process this data in real-time or near-real-time, which can place heavy demands on the data pipeline and the underlying infrastructure.

Another problem is ensuring that your data pipeline is fault-tolerant. If any portion of the pipeline fails, it can interrupt the entire process, leading to inaccurate forecasts or incomplete data. Using tools like Apache Kafka or AWS Kinesis, you can construct fault-tolerant pipelines that automatically recover from faults and continue processing data without losing information.

Data storage is another crucial feature in growing AI systems. As the amount of data rises, you need to store it in a way that makes it accessible and manageable. Cloud-based storage systems such as Amazon S3, Google Cloud Storage, or Azure Blob Storage can give scalable options for storing big volumes of data. However, you also need to think about data retrieval times and how to ensure that your models have fast access to the data they require.

4. Model Monitoring and Maintenance.

Once your AI model is in production, it is necessary to monitor its performance regularly. Even the well-designed models can decline with time, especially if the input data changes or new patterns arise. Monitoring your model helps you spot any flaws early on and take corrective action before they impair the system's performance.

There are various variables to monitor when scaling AI systems. First, you should track the model's accuracy and confirm that it is still making valid predictions. If the model starts to generate fewer accurate results, this can suggest that it has become old or that the underlying data distribution has changed. In such circumstances, retraining the model with new data can be necessary.

You should also check the system's performance in terms of speed and resource utilization. As the demand for your AI system develops, it may start demanding more processing resources. This can lead to reduced performance or increased expenditures. By monitoring resource utilization, you can find places where optimizations can be made.

AI systems also require frequent maintenance. Over time, data may need to be updated, or the model may need to be retrained to handle new forms of input. This procedure of regular maintenance guarantees that the system continues to work at its best.

Automated monitoring solutions can help you keep track of your AI system's health in real-time. Tools like TensorBoard, Prometheus, or Datadog let you visualize and track metrics like accuracy, latency, and resource utilization. By employing these tools, you can stay on top of the system's performance and verify that it continues to satisfy production needs.

5. Security and Privacy Concerns.

As AI systems scale, security and privacy become essential considerations. AI models routinely process sensitive data, and it is crucial to guarantee that this data is safeguarded from illegal access or misuse. Scaling your AI system entails installing security measures that secure both the data and the model itself.

One of the first stages in safeguarding an AI system is ensuring that sensitive data is encrypted both in transit and at rest. This ensures that even if data is intercepted or accessed by unauthorized people, it remains unreadable. Additionally, installing suitable authentication and access control systems can help prevent unauthorized individuals from accessing or modifying the system.

Another facet of security in AI systems is ensuring that the model itself is not vulnerable to adversarial assaults. Adversarial assaults entail changing the input data in ways that cause the model to generate inaccurate predictions. As AI systems scale and become more extensively utilized, the risk of such attacks increases. To avoid this risk, you can utilize approaches like adversarial training, where the model is subjected to adversarial samples during the training process to improve its robustness.

Privacy is another crucial factor, particularly when working with personal or sensitive data. Regulations like the General Data Protection Regulation (GDPR) in Europe mandate that AI systems handle personal data in a secure and privacy-conscious manner. Scaling your AI system must require taking the essential safeguards to comply with these standards and guarantee that users' privacy is maintained.

6. Cost Management and Scalability.

Finally, scaling an AI system also includes controlling expenditures effectively. AI models, especially large-scale ones, can be resource-intensive. From cloud computing resources to storage and data processing, the prices can quickly add up. It is crucial to have a strategy for scaling that balances performance with cost efficiency.

Cloud platforms generally offer pricing structures depending on the amount of resources utilized, so it's crucial to minimize the system's resource utilization to avoid excessive charges. This can involve employing spot instances for non-critical operations, optimizing the use of storage, or altering the level of parallelism in your distributed system to balance cost and performance.

By monitoring costs and altering your system's setup, you can ensure that your AI system remains scalable and economical as it expands. With the correct methodology, you can extend your AI system to handle larger datasets and more complicated tasks without compromising on performance or price.

Scaling AI systems for production involves a combination of technical competence, strategic planning, and continual monitoring. By optimizing the model, dividing the workload, managing data efficiently, and resolving security and privacy problems, you may design AI systems that are capable of handling real-world demands. As you grow in your AI journey, scaling your systems will become a vital skill, enabling you to deploy powerful, efficient, and reliable AI solutions in a wide range of applications.

6.3 Keeping Up with Emerging Trends in AI.

As you continue to polish your abilities and grow your experience in AI, it is crucial to stay educated about the ever-evolving landscape of artificial intelligence. The realm of AI is fast-paced and dynamic, with new breakthroughs and developments appearing often. Keeping up with developing trends ensures that your expertise remains up-to-date, and it lets you exploit the latest tools, methodologies, and technologies in your projects.

The speed at which AI evolves can sometimes feel daunting, but with the appropriate methods, you can remain ahead of the curve and continue to make substantial contributions to the field. Here are three major ways you can keep up with current trends and guarantee that your AI abilities stay relevant.

1. Follow leading research papers and journals.

One of the most efficient methods to stay informed about the latest breakthroughs in AI is by reading research papers and articles from top academic magazines. Research articles often provide cutting-edge insights, novel algorithms, and unique techniques that affect the future of AI.

Many notable conferences and magazines publish papers on the most recent breakthroughs in AI. Conferences like NeurIPS (Conference on Neural Information Processing Systems), ICML (International Conference on Machine Learning), and CVPR (Computer Vision and Pattern Recognition Conference) present the latest research and advancements in AI. These conferences give a venue for researchers, academics, and practitioners to communicate their findings and explore current trends in the field.

Academic magazines such as the Journal of Artificial Intelligence Research (JAIR) and

IEEE Transactions on Neural Networks and Learning Systems are other fantastic sources of in-depth research articles. By subscribing to or routinely checking these journals, you may keep on top of the latest research and grasp the most important directions in AI.

Many academic articles are now made freely available through sites like arXiv, an open-access repository where researchers upload their preprints. Reading these articles might be time-consuming, but it offers significant insight into how the field is going and where the next big breakthroughs may come from.

2. Stay Connected with AI Communities.

AI is a global discipline, and many of the most intriguing developments arise from online forums and social media platforms where practitioners, researchers, and enthusiasts share their opinions, insights, and discoveries. Staying involved with these communities can help you stay informed and establish a network of like-minded individuals.

Online platforms, including Reddit, Twitter, and LinkedIn, have active AI communities. On Reddit, for example, subreddits such as r/MachineLearning, r/ArtificialIntelligence, and r/deeplearning are loaded with conversations, news, and resources pertaining to the newest breakthroughs in AI. Twitter is another helpful site for following AI thought leaders, researchers, and industry experts who frequently post on developing trends, research papers, and developments in the area.

Participating in online forums and discussion groups allows you to ask questions, share your thoughts, and learn from others. Engaging with these groups might also introduce you to new ideas and trends that you would not have encountered through traditional methods.

Additionally, attending webinars, workshops, and online meetups can help you stay updated while also allowing you the opportunity to network with professionals and experts in AI. These events generally feature speakers from the vanguard of AI research and industry, providing you with useful knowledge and insights on current trends.

3. Engage with AI Blogs and Industry News.

In addition to research papers, AI blogs and industry news websites give current and accessible information on the latest trends, advancements, and applications of AI. Many AI specialists and organizations have blogs where they discuss recent advancements, emerging technology, and their significance for the industry.

Websites like Towards Data Science, Medium, and Analytics Vidhya contain a variety of articles, tutorials, and guidelines authored by both AI professionals and enthusiasts. These blogs address a wide range of subjects, from deep learning techniques and natural language processing improvements to ethical AI concerns and commercial applications. By reading these blogs, you can keep informed about both the academic and practical sides of AI.

Industry-specific news publications like TechCrunch, Wired, and MIT Technology Review also often include pieces concerning AI advancements and trends. These papers feature real-world applications of AI, illustrating how enterprises are utilizing AI to solve issues, streamline operations, and create new products and services.

By routinely monitoring these blogs and news sources, you may rapidly catch up on the newest breakthroughs and understand how AI is being implemented across numerous industries, from healthcare and banking to entertainment and transportation.

4. Participate in Online Courses and MOOCs.

Online classes and Massive Open Online Classes (MOOCs) are a wonderful method to keep up with current breakthroughs in AI while receiving hands-on experience with developing technology. These courses are generally prepared by major colleges and institutions, delivering in-depth training on cutting-edge issues in AI.

Platforms like Coursera, edX, Udacity, and DataCamp offer a wide choice of AI-related courses, from introductory to advanced levels. Many of these courses are taught by professors and industry specialists who are well-versed in the latest trends and breakthroughs in the sector. By taking these courses, you can learn about new algorithms, tools, and approaches that are driving the future of AI.

In addition to formal courses, sites like GitHub and Kaggle allow opportunities to engage with open-source AI projects and participate in data science competitions. These sites allow you to work on real-world AI challenges, collaborate with others, and demonstrate your expertise. By contributing to open-source projects or participating in competitions, you receive hands-on experience while also staying updated on the latest techniques and best practices in the field.

Many online courses and MOOCs are free or offer financial aid, making them an accessible choice for anyone wishing to increase their AI expertise without a substantial financial investment.

5. Experiment with Emerging Tools and Frameworks.

As AI continues to evolve, so do the tools and frameworks that make designing and deploying AI systems easier and more efficient. New libraries, platforms, and software development kits (SDKs) are continually being produced, giving faster performance, more functionality, and enhanced usability.

By experimenting with these new tools, you may remain ahead of the curve and incorporate the newest breakthroughs into your own AI initiatives. For example, TensorFlow, PyTorch, and Keras are prominent deep learning frameworks that continue to improve, bringing new capabilities and optimizations with each release. Similarly, platforms like OpenAI, Hugging Face, and Google Cloud AI offer pre-built models and APIs that allow you to easily install state-of-the-art AI solutions.

Many new tools also focus on enhancing accessibility and minimizing the complexity of working with AI. For instance, AutoML platforms are designed to automate portions of the machine learning pipeline, making it easier for non-experts to develop effective models. These tools are especially beneficial if you're trying to remain current on the latest AI capabilities without having to develop everything from scratch.

By keeping hands-on with emerging tools and frameworks, you ensure that you're well-equipped to work with the most modern technologies in AI, and you can incorporate these new tools into your own projects and processes.

6. Learn from Industry Leaders and Experts.

The AI field is shaped by the contributions of thought leaders, researchers, and industry specialists. Following these experts on social media, reading their books and blogs, and attending their lectures or speeches might give you significant insights on the path of AI development.

Prominent figures in AI, such as Yann LeCun, Geoffrey Hinton, Andrew Ng, and Demis Hassabis, are at the forefront of important advancements in deep learning, reinforcement learning, and AI research. Many of these specialists routinely express their thoughts and perspectives on the future of AI through interviews, podcasts, and public speeches. By learning from these leaders, you can obtain a deeper grasp of the difficulties and opportunities facing the AI sector.

Additionally, monitoring the work of firms that are driving innovation in AI—such as Google, DeepMind, Microsoft, and OpenAI—can keep you updated about the latest technology and applications. These firms typically provide research papers, blog posts, and product updates that highlight new trends and exhibit real-world AI applications.

7. Embrace a Continuous Learning Mindset.

Perhaps the most crucial method for keeping up with evolving trends in AI is to embrace a philosophy of constant learning. AI is a continually changing industry, and to stay relevant, you need to be open to new ideas and prepared to adapt to new technology. Whether you're attending conferences, reading research papers, or working on projects, always be open to improving your knowledge and honing your talents.

The capacity to learn new concepts, tools, and methodologies will keep you competitive in the quickly expanding area of AI. Don't be scared to make errors or confront hurdles along the way—these experiences are vital for growth. By keeping curious and committed to learning, you will continue to enhance your AI skills and keep up with the current advancements in the area.

Keeping up with emerging advancements in AI is vital for advancing your abilities and staying at the forefront of the field. By engaging with research papers, following AI communities, reading blogs and industry news, participating in online courses, playing with new tools, learning from experts, and maintaining an attitude of continuous learning, you can ensure that your AI expertise remains current and relevant. The world of AI will continue to grow, and by remaining educated, you'll be well-positioned to take advantage of new possibilities and contribute to the future of AI.

As we draw the final curtain on "The AI Scratch Code Playbook: A Beginner's Guide to Building Intelligent Systems," it is necessary to take a step back and reflect on the fantastic trip you've just been upon. You started your voyage with curiosity and a sense of wonder, and now, as you turn the last page, you find yourself equipped with a formidable toolset to design intelligent systems from the bottom up.

Think of your trip in this book as the foundation of a house. Every chapter, every concept you've learned, every line of code you've written, serves as a building block that will help your future initiatives in the field of AI. But, just like with any building job, the genuine worth of the house doesn't come from the materials alone; it comes from the creativity, passion, and vision that you, the builder, bring to it.

Building intelligent systems is not a task reserved for a select few. With the correct mindset and the tools you've learned, anyone with a drive to study may join the ranks of people influencing the future of technology. From the basics of programming to more sophisticated approaches in machine learning, neural networks, and deep learning, you now have a comprehensive and thorough understanding of AI principles. But this is just the beginning of your trip. The field of AI is broad, with unlimited prospects for growth and development.

Now that you have the foundational information, you have the power to begin experimenting with your own projects. The most fascinating element of designing intelligent systems lies in the application of the concepts you've learned. The greatest way to enhance your abilities is by practicing and experimenting, whether it's designing your first chatbot, constructing a recommendation system, or building a computer vision project. The options are unlimited, and with every new challenge, your abilities will increase and your confidence will soar.

However, don't be deceived into thinking that the path ahead will always be smooth. Building intelligent systems, like any worthwhile effort, takes perseverance, resilience, and a willingness to fail and try again. There will be instances when you feel stuck, when you're unclear of how to go or what the next move should be.

It's in these moments that you'll find the genuine beauty of problem-solving. When faced with a struggle, the most essential thing is to realize that every hurdle is an opportunity to learn, grow, and refine your talents. Failure is not the end but the beginning of new knowledge, a new plan, or a new way of thinking. With each setback, you acquire experience, and with every new lesson, you get closer to mastery.

As you continue to develop your abilities, remember that the field of AI is not only about designing systems that can execute tasks; it's about creating systems that can enhance lives. From healthcare to education, entertainment to economics, AI has the power to impact the world in significant ways. The systems you design may make a difference—whether it's enhancing the accessibility of information, helping people make better decisions, or even tackling global concerns. The potential for positive effect is boundless, and your contributions, no matter how tiny they may appear at first, can play a role in crafting a better future.

This book has provided you with the core knowledge needed to get started, but the learning never stops. The field of AI is continually growing, with new findings, approaches, and tools appearing every day. To remain on the cutting edge, it's crucial to stay curious and committed to lifelong learning. Continue to read, experiment, and challenge yourself. Connect with the worldwide AI community, engage in online forums, and attend conferences to stay current on the newest trends and breakthroughs. Seek mentors who can offer advice, share their experiences, and inspire you to reach new heights.

The path you've started is not only about coding and algorithms. It's about learning to think critically, solve problems creatively, and have a meaningful effect on the world. As you continue to develop your AI talents, you'll find that the most powerful systems you construct will be those that are guided by empathy, ethics, and a sense of duty. Remember that AI, like any tool, can be used for good or bad. It is up to you, the creator, to guarantee that the systems you design are used to enhance lives, promote fairness, and contribute to a just and equitable society.

In the chapters ahead, we've concentrated on offering a clear and accessible pathway to AI understanding, from the basics of programming to more sophisticated concepts like machine learning and neural networks. But we've also underlined the necessity of a mindset oriented around problem-solving, creativity, and ethical responsibility. These factors are equally as important as the technical abilities themselves because they will guide your decisions as you design and implement intelligent systems.

The methods and strategies in this book are designed to serve as stepping stones for your continued advancement in the field of AI. But it's not the tools that will define your success. It's your capacity to apply them in creative ways, to think critically about the challenges you're solving, and to preserve a feeling of interest and wonder about the world around you. AI is not simply an area of study—it's a way of thinking, a philosophy that inspires invention, curiosity, and the drive to change the world through technology.

As you stand at the brink of your future in AI, take a moment to reflect on how far you've come. From learning the foundations of coding to constructing your first models, you've already achieved something incredible. And now, with a firm understanding of the underlying ideas of AI, the future is yours to shape. The possibilities are boundless, and the journey ahead is one of perpetual growth, learning, and discovery.

In closing, remember that AI is not just for IT gurus or researchers—it's for everyone. You have the tools, the knowledge, and the will to make your mark in this exciting and fast-evolving sector. Whether you're designing intelligent systems for personal projects, entering the field as an AI expert, or building the next big idea, the journey you've begun is just the beginning. Continue to push limits, think beyond the box, and continuously strive for growth.

And above all, remember that every step you take in the world of AI puts you closer to becoming a creator, a problem solver, and a change maker. So, take that next step with confidence, and let your journey into the world of AI be one of discovery, transformation, and unlimited opportunity. The world needs intellectuals like you—people who are eager to construct the future with intelligence, creativity, and purpose. The tools you need are in your hands, and the adventure is just beginning. What will you develop next?